ADVANCE PRAISE

"FightBack Now shares helpful insights on how to bring together diverse minds and cultures for meaningful innovation."

EVA KAILI
MEMBER, EUROPEAN PARLIAMENT
CHAIR, EUROPEAN PARLIAMENT COMMITTEE
FOR THE FUTURE OF SCIENCE AND TECHNOLOGY

"A must-read primer for leaders of big companies and society considering taking an entrepreneurial journey and creating new sources of growth from existing assets."

RALF BELUSA
MANAGING DIRECTOR, HAPAG-LLOYD AG

"Incumbents across the economy have watched the rise of Big Tech with fascination, envy, and trepidation, but have often struggled to formulate a response. *Fightback Now* offers practical advice for firms to respond by helping them take advantage of their strong existing assets. I found the advice for corporate venture-building to be particularly relevant: get the right incentives, align culture, connect to the 'mother ship', and ensure regulatory compliance with as light a touch as possible."

GEOFFREY PARKER
PROFESSOR, DARTMOUTH COLLEGE, VISITING SCHOLAR
AND FELLOW, MIT INITIATIVE ON THE DIGITAL ECONOMY

"As we work our way through the havoc wreaked by the pandemic, the tools of purposeful innovation will be central to recovery efforts. *FightBack Now* offers a wealth of new ideas and solid thinking about how to move forward."

RITA MCGRATH
PROFESSOR OF MANAGEMENT,
COLUMBIA BUSINESS SCHOOL

"As an impact entrepreneur, I wholeheartedly agree with a core thesis of this book: that we can fight climate change by building companies with sustainable visions. From commerce to mobility, I am convinced that every business sector must take actions today to protect our planet now! *FightBack Now* outlines a clear vision for how this can be put into practice at scale."

LAWRENCE LEUSCHNER
CEO AND CO-FOUNDER, TIER MOBILITY

"We need radical innovations to tackle complex societal challenges that the crisis exposed. *FightBack Now* makes an important point: large corporations need to play a much stronger role if we are to deliver these radical innovations and, ultimately, make the next normal more sustainable."

IVANKA VISNJIC
PROFESSOR, ESADE BUSINESS SCHOOL

"The insurance industry is one of the key enablers to human progress. As society changes, so do the underlying risks. New approaches to leveraging our corporate assets and partly disrupting our market models will ensure our role in a transforming society. But we need tons of new capabilities and a dramatic increase in speed. *FightBack Now* illustrates why and how corporate venture building can help accelerate this transition."

OLIVER SCHOELLER
CEO, GOTHAER ALLGEMEINE

"The sustainability market is challenging, and we therefore need a diversity of leaders to join our mission. *FightBack Now* is the book for a new movement of impact driven leaders."

ANNA ALEX
CO-FOUNDER AND CCO, PLANETLY

"Toyota has pledged to transform itself from a car manufacturer into an integrated mobility company by 2030. We know that we are not going to do that alone but by joining forces with people coming from different horizons. *FightBack Now* shows ways in which such new kinds of collaboration can work and would benefit society as a whole."

ALAIN UYTTENHOVEN
CEO, TOYOTA DEUTSCHLAND GMBH

"The monumental challenges of our times coincide with the necessity of reconfiguring the institutional framework of our society, on a global scale. With its emphasis on creatively combining entrepreneurial innovation with the shaping power of responsible global corporations, *FightBack Now* sets out to serve as a key enabler of what needs to be done."

ROLAND DEISER
FOUNDER AND EXECUTIVE CHAIRMAN,
CENTER FOR THE FUTURE OF ORGANIZATION
AT THE DRUCKER SCHOOL OF MANAGEMENT,
AND AUTHOR, *DESIGNING THE SMART ORGANIZATION*

"*FightBack Now* is all about harnessing existing assets through the power of digital technologies for a more sustainable future and more resilient societies."

ANDREAS KUNZE
FOUNDER AND CEO, KONUX

"As we use all the technologies at our disposal to define the new normal, we must bear in mind the deeper purpose. It is not improving efficiency or fuelling economic growth. As important as these are, the true mission is to enable strong human connections, to empower culture as an important element in society and to allow us to lead the purposeful and enriching lives we all long for. *FightBack Now* is a call to action for the impactful business innovation that we desperately need now."

DMITRIY AKSYONOV
CHAIRMAN OF THE BOARD OF DIRECTORS,
RDI GROUP

"In a post-pandemic world, *FightBack Now* calls on large organizations to deploy their assets differently to allow us to respond with more agility through digital technologies and platform business models."

SANGEET PAUL CHOUDARY
RENOWNED PLATFORM ECONOMIST
AND STRATEGIST

"Defining the new normal is a responsibility for all of us. We cannot just leave socially impactful work in the hands of the public and non-governmental sectors. As *FightBack Now* beautifully points out, it is just as much a responsibility of the big corporations to drive meaningful structural change to help achieve the UN's sustainable development goals."

ANDREAS RICKERT
CEO AND FOUNDER, PHINEO

"Corporate innovation requires a radical rethink as we enter a new world increasingly mediated by digital ecosystems. Western industry, in particular, needs to create a new dialogue with investors, look to the longer term, adopt new metrics and co-opt new entrepreneurial talent. *FightBack Now* provides a coherent blueprint for doing this."

MICHAEL G. JACOBIDES
PROFESSOR OF STRATEGY,
LONDON BUSINESS SCHOOL

"*FightBack Now* shows how established corporations can put creative people in the driving seat to accelerate meaningful innovation."

SASCHA PALLENBERG
HEAD OF DIGITAL TRANSFORMATION, DAIMLER AG

"As we move out of this pandemic, we must make sure that we keep our momentum, so that we will meet future challenges being better prepared. This is what *FightBack Now* is all about."

ANNE BERNER
ENTREPRENEUR AND INVESTOR, AND FORMER MINISTER, FINLAND

"We as ecosystem leaders, and we as a community, should not support any entrepreneurship that is not based on responsible, sustainable development and with very clear rules and very clear impact, aims and purposes. *FightBack Now* is a call to action for entrepreneurial social value creation."

PLAMEN RUSSEV
FOUNDER AND EXECUTIVE CHAIRMAN, WEBIT.FOUNDATION

"Change is the (only) stable and guaranteed variable moving forward. It's not a bug. It's going to become the norm. It's not only a need and fit for the largest corporates; sustainable change spreads way beyond. Leaders and CEOs are now being required to put social responsibility into action. From upgrades to new services and products, we have the responsibility to build increased value and create new jobs. *Fightback Now* is the crucible for this urgently needed transformation."

LIONEL PAILLET
ADVISOR AND PREVIOUSLY GENERAL MANAGER,
NEST, GOOGLE, APPLE

"Every crisis instigates an entrepreneurship boom. A whole new generation of entrepreneurs will emerge from this unfortunate humanitarian and economic crisis. After all, necessity is the mother of all invention. If you want to be part of this new breed of thinking, *FightBack Now* is a great place to start."

GERARD GRECH
CEO, TECH NATION

Published by
LID Publishing Limited
The Record Hall, Studio 304,
16-16a Baldwins Gardens,
London EC1N 7RJ, UK

info@lidpublishing.com
www.lidpublishing.com

A member of:

businesspublishersroundtable.com

Printed in the United States
ISBN: 978-1-911671-33-6

Cover design: Ziar Khosrawi
Page design: Caroline Li

FIGHTBACK NOW

LEVERAGING YOUR ASSETS TO SHAPE THE NEW NORMAL

FELIX STAERITZ

DR SVEN JUNGMANN

MADRID | MEXICO CITY | LONDON
NEW YORK | BUENOS AIRES
BOGOTA | SHANGHAI | NEW DELHI

CONTENTS

ACKNOWLEDGMENTS

Especially in 2020, life has been pretty intense, for us and for those around us. Thank you to our families – Felix's wife, Kamelia, and son, Kian, and his parents, Simone and Christian, and Sven's Anne and Friedhelm, Dirk and Anke – and to all our friends.

We are also grateful for:

The relentless support of our partners at FoundersLane, Andreas and Michael, and all the team who contributed day and night to this book.

Their contribution, in terms of sparring, foreword, cases, quotes, feedback and challenging us, has been massive. Thank you to all who have supported us on this journey and given their backing to the *FightBack* book, to the community and to whatever is to come.

One aspect of writing this book that has surprised and delighted us is the amazing level of interest, enthusiasm and cooperation we've met from the top business people, entrepreneurs and even political leaders we've been talking to.

So we are really appreciative of the business leaders' perspectives of Thomas Ogilvie (board member, DHL Group), Jonathan Larsen (CIO of Ping An), Sascha Pallenberg (Head of Digital, Daimler), Karthik Suri (formerly of GE Digital), Gisbert Rühl (CEO of Klöckner), Marcus Wallenberg (Chair of SEB bank, Saab AB and FAM AB; Vice Chair of Investor AB),

Dr Rahmyn Kress (former CDO of Henkel), Alain Uyttenhoven (MD of Toyota Europe), Gert De Winter (CEO of Baloise), Alex Manson (CEO, Standard Chartered Ventures), Peter Albiez (MD of Pfizer Germany), Boris Marte (Head of the Erste Bank Innovation Hub) Lars Zimmerman (MD of public.io), Oliver Schoeller (CEO of Gothaer), Anne Berner (investor, board member and former minister) and Gerard Grech (CEO of Tech Nation).

Spread through these pages you'll find recent, fascinating interviews with world-class entrepreneurs like Claire Novorol and Daniel Nathrath (co-founders of Ada Health), Ida Tin (co-founder of Clue), Anna Alex (co-founder of Planetly), Nicolas Brusson (founder of BlaBlaCar), Rolf Schrömgens (co-founder of Trivago), Markus Fuhrmann (co-founder of Delivery Hero), Plamen Russev (founder of Webit Foundation) and Alexander Wennergren Helm (Chairman of the Board at Doktor24).

We have also had fascinating inputs from leaders in academia, politics and non-governmental organizations, like Eva Kaili (European Parliament), Martina Larkin (World Economic Forum), Geoff Parker (MIT Initiative on the Digital Economy), Linda Hill (Harvard Business School), Brigitte Mohn (board member, Bertelsmann), Sebastian Borek (Founders Foundation), Rita McGrath (Columbia Business School), Ivanka Visnjic (ESADE), Michael G. Jacobides (London Business School), Anant Jani (University of Oxford), Steven Tebbe and Laurent Babikian (CDP), Roland Deiser (Executive Chairman at Center for the Future of Organization, Drucker School of Management), Sebastian Copeland (polar explorer, author and activist) and Torsten Thiele (founder of the Global Ocean Trust).

We want to say a very warm thank you to the following people, but there are so many more. Thank you to Ziar Khosrawi, Cain Rothe, Frank Van Beuzekom, Tim Thonhauser-Röhrich, Ian Shircore, Nikola Likov, Rita Maier, Andrej Henkler, Adam Mitchell-Heggs, Gustav Wakeus, Andreas Ringman Uggla, Richy Ugwu, Peter Borchers, Tomasz Bilakiewicz, Bradley Franco, Manuel Mandler, Alexander Bockelmann, Patrick Wirth, Mark Cliffe, Sangeet Paul Choudary and, of course, all our friends and colleagues at the World Economic Forum. We would also like to thank Jochen Wilms, Alex Uglov, Anthony Roberts, Christian Rebernik, Gernot Przestrzelski, Jürgen Furian, Antonia Becker, Fabio Hotic, Lionel Paillet, Andrej Henkler, Cliff Hinrichs, Chasan Mochament, Andreas Aspoeck, Andreas Kunze, Rodrigo Freire de Sa, Carolin Lessoued and the Openers team, Alexej Habinski, Ulrich Faisst, Ralf Belusa, Michael Meehan, Wolfgang Gründinger, Johanna Lehmann, Lisa von Rabenau, Deemah AlYahya and Dmitriy Aksyonov.

We're indebted to them all for their time and their ideas, and for making *FightBack* even more than the book we hoped it would be.

KEY TERMS

ASSET CLASS

Asset classes are groupings of investments that exhibit similar characteristics and are subject to the same regulation. Historically, the four main asset classes have been cash, equities, bonds and tangible assets such as property.

Analysts increasingly cite investments in commodities, venture capital, corporate venture building, hedge funds and cryptocurrencies as important examples of alternative asset classes.

CORPORATE VENTURE BUILDING (CVB)

Corporate venture building is an asset class based on a systematic process for building new businesses with business models that are substantially different from those of the parent organization.

CVB is a hybrid approach that employs entrepreneurial methods to maximize the leverage available via the incumbent's existing assets – industry expertise, plant, data, reputation and so on – and create a portfolio of aligned but independent new businesses.

CVB is not limited to building new businesses from scratch. It may also achieve its aims by buying or partnering. Success depends on choosing a suitable digital operating model and, in particular, on the establishment of an Entrepreneurial

Growth Board to guide and manage the setting up, financing and growth of the new ventures.

ENTREPRENEURIAL OPERATING MODEL (EOM)

The Entrepreneurial Operating Model establishes the relationship between the corporation and the new digital businesses and provides the essential channel for frank, unambiguous two-way communication.

The EOM is a structured framework for the management of the hybrid organization (core business and new business units), ensuring that corporate venture building and other investment activity (such as M&A and corporate venture capital initiatives) are always aligned with its overall strategic objectives.

ENTREPRENEURIAL GROWTH BOARD (EGB)

The Entrepreneurial Growth Board has the authority to make crucial buy/build/partner and investment decisions and governs how and when each new business unit can access and leverage the assets of the core organization. It acts as a steering committee, controls the strategy and oversees all new digital value creation activities.

The EGB is made up of senior people from both sides of the hybrid organization, plus experienced entrepreneurs brought in from the outside world. It forms the essential bridge between the corporate board and the new ventures, both at a practical operational level and in terms of reconciling cultural tensions.

In some regulated industries it may be necessary to set up more than one board to meet compliance requirements.

WHITE SPACE GARAGE

White spaces represent uncontested market gaps that offer the potential for rapid growth or major social impact. Identifying them pinpoints important new opportunities to create value by leveraging new technologies and business models.

The White Space Garage is the notional 'place of safety' where customers' deepest needs are explored and new ideas can be conceived, researched, mocked up, validated and, if necessary, killed off, at high speed in an atmosphere of uninhibited creativity.

FOREWORD

Martina Larkin is a member of the World Economic Forum's Executive Committee and its head of Europe and Eurasia. Based on her role and expertise, she focuses mainly on the situation in Europe. But you will certainly find common themes here, wherever you are based.

The World Economic Forum hits the headlines every January when nearly 3,000 participants, including the world's heads of state, CEOs, economists and NGO organizers gather for the flagship Davos meeting in the Swiss Alps. This year's attendees included Christine Lagarde (President, European Central Bank), Greta Thunberg (climate and environmental activist), Angela Merkel (Federal Chancellor of Germany) and Donald Trump (President of the United States of America). But WEF's main work is done out of the spotlight, year-round, and involves producing a wide range of research reports and driving international initiatives on urgent global issues like health, education, climate change, the fight against corruption and responses to social and technological change.

The worldwide crisis triggered by Covid-19 is without modern parallel. It is a defining moment and we will all be dealing with the consequences for many years to come. The exact extent of the change is not yet clear, but one thing we know is that the pandemic will fast-forward innovation even more. It will accelerate the technological changes already under way and provide a great range of new opportunities for many digital businesses. It will also accentuate the need for every business to strengthen its digital dimension.

The crisis has revealed that, in today's rapidly changing world, our assumptions about business and society and the complex systems that govern our trade and institutions are looking increasingly fragile, outdated and not fit for purpose. We must act with a great sense of urgency to move out of this crisis and reset our global systems. The good news is that we have significant technologies at our disposal to develop new and meaningful solutions to cope with these emerging challenges. Fostering a healthy and thriving innovation ecosystem is a major element in resetting the current systems.

At the Forum, we convened experts and leaders in the digital economy to identify the four key catalysts that must be addressed to enable Europe to play a full part in the innovation race. There are four main drivers that will also be of interest to leaders in other parts of the world:

1. We need to be much more strategic about the industries we focus on. We need to create much better cross-sector innovation strategies and platforms for high-performing industries like healthcare, the financial sector and manufacturing.

2. Data is vital, and Europe needs to take the lead when it comes to data governance. Data is the new oil, and we are well positioned to change the dynamics when it comes to the governance of data around the world. We need to develop a healthy and durable system, based on European values and principles, but also a marketplace for data where relevant data can be shared and aggregated for research, policy-making and better decision-making.

3. Talent is becoming a key asset. In fact, talent is now winning out over capital, because capital is becoming much more abundant and mobile. Talent is where you can differentiate yourself and be more competitive, so those companies and countries that can attract, keep and develop talent will be tomorrow's winners. And we should certainly be encouraging more female entrepreneurship. Only one in 20 start-ups has a female founder – a clear sign that we are wasting a lot of innovation potential and a lot of opportunities for growth.

4. The other asset that can work in our favour is the large amount of public sector procurement, across Europe, that could be allocated in much more strategic ways, with more emphasis on the digital industries and growing the digital economy. This has been a key factor in China and, to some extent – in defence procurement, for example – in the US. In Europe, for instance, it could potentially provide a new impetus towards creating a positive environment for digital innovation.

This crisis is showing us the importance of investing in technology and innovation (scientific R&D and STEM skills) and it highlights the need to invest in maximizing the benefits and minimizing the risks to society of the Fourth Industrial Revolution, including innovations in tech-public goods, such as public health, global data platforms and early warning systems. National economies, international relations and global supply chains are all being affected by the Fourth Industrial Revolution, in ways that create serious risks but also immense opportunities for business and society. The platform economy is here, but we don't yet know how to live and operate in this new world. We need systems-changing technology and governance breakthroughs for a shared prosperity within the boundaries of our global commons.

We must, at the same time, invest in structural changes to respond to today's climate challenges, as is being done, for example, with the European Green Deal. As we develop recovery strategies, rather than going back to previous flawed systems and models, we have a unique opportunity to rethink our economies, international relations, institutions and the way our societies work. We must develop a greener, more digital and more inclusive future – one that addresses the jobs crisis and skills shortages while accelerating towards our net zero emissions targets and sustainable development goals.

All of this has to come with strong leadership and decisive action. Above all, it has to happen now. We need speed. We need scale. We need strategic direction. We need a new approach to building digital businesses so that we can make best use of our technologies to solve the big challenges that lie ahead of us.

In this timely and thought-provoking book, Felix and Sven provide great input for a broader discussion and a blueprint to act in the business and political world. At its core lies the notion of a new asset class that leverages existing assets and unites 'hybrid leaders' to build transformative digital businesses with social purpose. But no tool will help us if we can't muster the leadership and sense of urgency needed to become more proactive in mastering the tests of our times.

ABOUT THE AUTHORS

Entrepreneurs want to change the world. That's how they are. They are born activists, permanently, restlessly dissatisfied with the status quo, whether it's in business or in society. They're impatient for change and intolerant of habits, traditions and assumptions that exist just because "That's how things have always been".

They get their ideas from everything around them – from what they see, hear, read, get frustrated by, dream or imagine. And once they've got an idea, they want to try it out. That's because, to the true entrepreneur, an idea that goes nowhere is not worth having.

FoundersLane co-founder Felix Staeritz is a successful entrepreneur, investor, husband and father. He started his first entrepreneurial activities at the age of 16, when he arrived back in Germany after a year in the United States. The entrepreneurial spirit bit him, and he stayed bitten. Around the time he finished high school, near Dresden, he received funding from businesses, the European Union and German foundations to pursue his first mission of improving the educational system.

Felix is a mission-driven entrepreneur. Despite the success of his first entrepreneurial activities, his parents insisted he should go on to university. "You never know what'll happen to you, and a university degree will give you a good life," they said. After studying in Europe, the US and Asia, and gaining experience in strategy consulting, he continued his mission-driven entrepreneurial activities and has since founded successful start-ups and digital platforms, such as KochAbo/ MarleySpoon, ShareTheMeal, Solytic and many more. He is also a business angel and an investor in Cavalry, an early-stage venture capital fund, and Profectus Capital, a private equity fund. He is the co-founder and CEO of FoundersLane, a founders-driven corporate venture builder with a focus on health and climate-related industries, operating in Europe, MENA and Asia.

With more than 20 years' experience of building businesses up to IPO, he is also a board member of the World Economic Forum's Digital Leaders community and a member of the Forbes Technology Council. Felix has also written the bestselling book *FightBack* and established the FightBack initiative, a multi-stakeholder platform that forms strategic alliances between the most relevant corporations, decision-makers and supporters in Europe to join forces and co-create sustainable solutions to the massive societal and economic challenges of climate and health.

Back in 2013, Felix was put in touch with Sven Jungmann, who was supposed to be helping him find an apartment in Cologne, where Felix had moved to set up the German HQ of a company. They never actually met, but they stayed in contact. Five years later, Sven posted that he was about to go on a new journey in his professional life, after having been Chief Medical Officer at a digital corporate venture of Helios, then Europe's largest hospital provider. He had begun a promising career as a hands-on doctor, but had become so frustrated with various countries' health systems (after gaining front-line experience in Germany, France,

Spain, South Africa, Brazil and Kenya) that he made a big commitment to himself. He would go all out to unleash the power of digital technologies in the healthcare space, to make our health systems so awesome that even he would want to return to work at the bedside. It was time for him to take a step closer to this ambition and switch from a management role into real digital entrepreneurship. Sven had already launched an e-commerce company and a lending firm and studied healthcare entrepreneurship at Cambridge. Now he was keen to do more. Felix, always intrigued by healthcare, saw Sven's post announcing his new move and contacted him to go on a journey together. For both, it seemed the obvious thing to do.

The authors had led very different lives, with very different experiences and professional backgrounds. But they both had the same goal – to make a positive impact on the planet by creating and scaling new digital solutions. When they met, it seemed natural that they would join forces on their mission to help solve the big challenges of humanity. Their personal narrative echoes a recurring theme in this book: the way groundbreaking change requires new alliances across disciplines and industries, demanding constant unlearning and a continuous reinventing of oneself.

In just a few years, FoundersLane has helped build various new digital businesses together with powerful established corporations in Europe, Asia and the MENA region. Some of them are well known, such as Solytic, the world's leading and fastest-growing solar marketplace, and alley.de, a personalized digital patient guide for people with hip problems. This has only been possible because of the many people who had faith in the journey and mission of FoundersLane and FightBack.

Being in love with a journey creates an urge to share it. The deeper desire behind this book is to nurture people's curiosity about building new ventures. It's to let you know that it is time, if you haven't done so already, to wake up your inner entrepreneur and leverage your assets through digital business models with corporate venture building, a new asset class. The challenges that lie ahead for humanity are complex. A new approach is needed to fight back. As you will learn, it starts with you and your commitment to master what will emerge, post-Covid, as the new normal.

FELIX STAERITZ AND DR SVEN JUNGMANN

BERLIN, SEPTEMBER 2020

PREFACE

We wrote this second version of *FightBack, Leverage your Assets to Master the New Normal*, because we believe humanity is currently punching far below its weight. We have created incredible technologies that are at our everyday disposal. Yet we've also come to realize, sometimes painfully, just how interdependent our systems are and how much we struggle to respond to crises in a coordinated, united way.

This book is being written in early summer 2020, in the middle of the Covid-19 crisis. At this time, people around the world are still speculating about what will happen next. There probably won't be a safe vaccine ready for mass use before 2022, and we foresee that global growth will be stunted for several years to come. But we believe we have formidable tools at our disposal – not just to cope with this situation, but to recreate our world so we come out of this stronger and more inventive. We will need that, because humanity is probably going to be encountering more Covid-like disasters in the very near future.

As entrepreneurs, we are passionate about solving challenges through continuous experimentation, in search of the solutions that will define and shape the new normal. As human beings, we are well aware that a 10% change in our behaviour will not lead to the results we all need. Here, we've set out to describe how corporate venture building, a new asset class, can help us become more systematic in leveraging existing assets through digital technologies and aligning the inventive forces of entrepreneurs and corporations around a big, hairy, audacious common goal.

The previous edition of *FightBack* was written by Felix Staeritz and Simon Torrance and published at the end of 2019. It looked at the power and capabilities of platforms and new business models and explored the potential of a new approach to creating new businesses that could be adopted by large organizations wishing to inject digital know-how and entrepreneurial flair into their innovation efforts. In the few months that have passed since its publication, the world has changed abruptly, with the Covid-19 crisis highlighting, more than ever, the need for both government and business to respond creatively and energetically to the threats and challenges facing us. However painful, it has been a learning opportunity – and we feel our recent experience, alongside the feedback we have received from our readers, has given us many new and important insights that amply justify the effort of writing a new edition, with a special emphasis on the urgent global issues of health and climate change.

As before, some readers may feel our title, *FightBack*, is either too belligerent or too emotional. We don't think it is. We are facing serious problems that are very complex, because they include a lot of scientific uncertainty, that require humans to change their behaviour and that are rooted in deeply regulated markets with massive market failures. This is well outside the comfort zone of any normal start-up.

There is a need to respond with a strong sense of urgency, because we really are in a race against time – as Covid-19 has already made clear. As entrepreneurs, we see opportunities in every crisis. This one is an opportunity to learn a lot about our systems' shortcomings and to define the new normal. But let's not see ourselves as victims. Let's take constructive action together, with concerted efforts to work hard for the changes we, as the human race, need, if we are to survive and thrive.

We believe that everything we've written so far was already true, long before the pandemic hit us. But the coronavirus has certainly accelerated many key trends and made them more palpable.

At its core, this book is about the shared experiences of many business leaders, academics and entrepreneurs around how corporations can most effectively build new digital models to make the most of their existing assets. But you will probably be surprised to see that we talk about seemingly unrelated topics, such as the macro challenges society is facing, the different mindsets of innovators and the potential of today's new platform business models. We know some of the connections aren't immediately obvious, but we are confident that you will come round to seeing these issues as relevant and connected, if you don't see them that way already.

This new edition of *FightBack* is needed because of the new realities we are facing. It is largely focused on the urgent problems of health and climate, which may seem, at first glance, to be far removed from your industry. But you may want to think again about that. These two areas are particularly suited to the corporate venture building approach and offer many profitable business opportunities, as well as being vitally important for our children's future.

This is not a scientific dissertation. It is provocative, because it needs to be. It is a call to arms for all of us as we move into a time of unprecedented challenges. If, after this, you feel engaged, wanting to do something concrete that's within your reach, then we'll know that the long nights spent writing this book were well worth the effort.

INTRODUCTION

COVID-19 IS THE ALARM CALL
WE'VE BEEN DREADING

How many new friendships have you made as a result of social distancing? For us, living in Berlin and Vienna, local WhatsApp groups have rekindled the kind of neighbourhood spirit you would normally see in much smaller towns. Through online dinners, we have met friends of friends from all over the world – people we would probably not have got to know quite so easily under other circumstances. When we spoke to Mark Cliffe, global head of the New Horizons Hub at ING, he invited us to try an interesting thought experiment: imagine how you would have experienced this crisis without Zoom and WhatsApp calls, the internet, streaming, online shops and all the rest of the connections that have kept us in touch with each other.

NUMBER OF DAILY USERS IN ZOOM MEETINGS (IN MILLIONS)

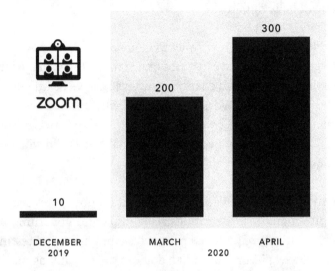

Video chat's explosive growth during Covid-19

STATISTA, 2020

"Our technologies saved us from a cataclysmic collapse in society. Without mobiles, computers and the internet, we would have fared much worse," he said.

But there is a massive gap between our technological capabilities and what we made of them in our efforts to cope with this crisis. This gap is the result of inertia, of inefficiencies in the ways we orchestrate progress, and it is a factor in the human tragedies that are unfolding now.

This new coronavirus has held a mirror up to our lives, showing them up in pitiless detail. It's a mirror we can't resist gazing at – and it's one that has highlighted parts of ourselves we've chosen to ignore for far too long. At the same time, though, it has revealed positive aspects of ourselves that we had almost stopped believing in.

Covid-19 has brought tragedy to many of us. Some have lost loved ones. Others have lost jobs or had to fire their staff just to give their companies a chance of survival. We've heard people call this pandemic 'World War C'. And who knows what is to come? This may just be the beginning. Peering forward from mid-2020, we cannot begin to guess what this world will look like even six months ahead.

By and large, this deadly virus found us poorly prepared, despite many prior warnings. Hospitals and governments quickly ran out of personal protective equipment and testing kits. We saw pictures of Italian doctors wearing diving masks and Spanish medics taping bin bags round their necks to try to cut the risk of infection. People hoarded flour, paracetamol tablets and toilet paper. When national governments geared up their efforts and began purchasing millions of items of protective equipment, missing shipments and counterfeiting scams made daily headlines.

There was a terrible sense of helplessness, coupled with a great deal of finger-pointing – 'external attribution', as the psychologists call it. The problem was blamed on some other nations' bad faith, or on government inertia, or on society's attitudes. For many months we didn't even know the most basic facts, like how many people had been infected.

HOW DID IT COME TO THIS?

For most countries, the lack of preparedness should be a cause for concern. What had happened to them? Their grandparents rebuilt great cities and strong economies from the rubble of World War II. They introduced high levels of social welfare and collaborated to bring age-old enemies together in a unique union of diverse nations, with high productivity and a leading role in global innovation. And yet, compared with other regions of the world, they seemed to have settled into comfortable complacency and lost their drive to keep up with the moment. Many have been happily coasting in 'innovation limbo', doing what was just good enough to stay relevant, rather than pushing the boundaries of what's possible.

Europe's companies still account for one-quarter of the world's industrial R&D, but they lacked the ability to quickly produce simple face masks or Covid-testing components at scale. They were missing data measurement and interoperability standards to ensure swift responses where help was needed most. It took a while until we saw dedicated responses by leaders in the public and private sectors. As a result, we witnessed a free-for-all, rather than compassionate mutual support. Apparently, it takes a shock like the Covid pandemic, a classic example of scholar Nassim Nicholas Taleb's theory of Black Swans (high-impact, once-in-a-lifetime events) to test a society's agility.

Even before the arrival of the new coronavirus, though, we were among those warning traditional businesses of the need to wake up and respond to a more predictable series of revolutionary changes in business and society.

As our friends at the World Economic Forum have been highlighting for several years, we are in the early stages of a digital revolution – what the WEF calls the Fourth Industrial Revolution – that will be far-reaching in its implications and disruptive in its impact on existing businesses, societies and structures. This Fourth Industrial Revolution is a change that will transform the way our companies, governments, utilities and even transport and healthcare systems operate, whether we like it or not. But there will be tremendous opportunities alongside the threats, and we need to focus on how we can make the most of them.

> "There is this myth, especially in the corporate world, that governments are not agile, that they are too slow, too bureaucratic. But I also know how corporates work, and I've worked with a lot of big corporates over the last few years. All big organizations tend to have the same issues. It doesn't really matter whether you are a private company or a government agency."
>
> LARS ZIMMERMANN
> **MANAGING DIRECTOR AT PUBLIC,
> A GOVTECH VC/ACCELERATOR**

For the world's richer countries, at least, this is not just a matter of overcoming the forces of habit, convention and inertia. It is primarily a moral imperative that insists that every nation should use its capabilities and assets, earned over centuries of industrialization, to find new ways to meet the needs of humanity and our planet and create a prosperous and enjoyable future we can all share. Eva Kaili, a Greek member of the European Parliament, stresses the need for political leadership: "The current crisis is giving us new impulses for action and to gain the trust of society. But we must not focus narrowly on individual problems. I think the Green Deal and sustainability, in general, are crucial for us. They will affect the air we breathe, the food we eat and the employment we have — all of which touch our lives in meaningful ways. We have to look at this holistically."

These are the immediate challenges we should be concerned about. On a grander scale, as Covid-19 has viciously reminded us, there are bigger issues to confront, issues that demand the full-scale mobilization of all the forces we can bring to bear – from governments to businesses and from NGOs to citizens' initiatives.

We may have been temporarily distracted, but even when the coronavirus crisis is behind us, we are going to have to orchestrate immediate, forceful and determined international action to prevent the imminent catastrophe of climate breakdown. One of the few obvious bonuses of this horrifying pandemic is the stark reminder it has provided that the most urgent and deadly problems cannot be contained within national borders or tackled without global cooperation.

Covid-19 has shone an uncomfortable light on the Western nations' weaknesses. Have they become complacent? Have they lost their resilience, their ingenuity and their ability to improvise and innovate quickly? Have they been taking their heritage of peace, freedom, education, social security and health for granted?

The West has a long history of inventiveness and creativity. Europe, for example, has many world-leading companies that are seldom recognized outside the niche markets in which they operate. These hidden champions, however, have often been biased towards the more traditional industry sectors – towards hardware, rather than software, and traditional pharmaceuticals, rather than biotechnology – and they've been slow to respond to the next generation of frontier technologies. They have fine scientists and good public sector research, but they have fallen behind in key areas such as artificial intelligence, quantum computing, synthetic biology and genomics.

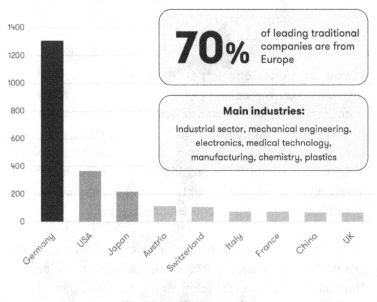

World-leading expertise

ADAPTED FROM SIMON KUCHER AND PARTNERS

There is a lot of catching up to do, but there is not too much time for finger-pointing. As we'll discuss, leaders around the world, including in Africa, Latin America, Oceania and practically every other part of the globe, will need to make their contributions to pre-empting and solving the problems facing humanity.

As Ivanka Visnjic of Spain's ESADE Business School, a 'Top 40 Under 40' professor, warns: "We absolutely need radical innovation that does not just solve individual customer needs, but attacks deeply rooted systemic problems. This crisis has shown up a lot of challenges to the healthcare ecosystem that we need to address. We can also use this as a thought experiment about what a climate crisis would look like."

WE NEED A SENSE OF URGENCY

"What surprises me in the webinars I give now to business leaders," Linda Hill of Harvard Business School told us recently, "is that many people start by asking me 'Do you think innovation matters now?' This is a curious question. It suggests that people often think that innovation is something extra, something special, not what you do when you're trying to survive. Yet it is precisely within this unprecedented challenge that we need new kinds of solutions. This means that we need to gather new teams and operate in ways that will allow us to come up with those new solutions."

Every industry, bar none, is ripe for disruption. It's just a matter of time. Every society is being affected by the digital revolution, in countless large and small ways.

Successful companies and resilient societies have two things in common: the ability to recognize changes in demand and the opportunities they bring, and the ability to spot and address threats. Until recently, most business leaders saw their role largely in relation to their own industries – their markets, their supply chains and their competitors.

Covid-19 has made us look up and see the larger picture, showing us all too clearly how powerful forces outside the market can be, and that aggressive start-ups don't have a monopoly on disruption. We live in an interconnected and potentially dangerous world, capable of changing at breakneck speed, in which every organization and every individual needs to become more agile and inventive.

We need to think fast and act quickly. Corporate and government leaders need to find ways to co-opt the tech entrepreneurs and digital disrupters and get them on their side, working with them, rather than against them. We all need a new asset class to overcome our inertia and fight back.

The coronavirus tragedy may at least restore our sense of urgency. For most of us in the affluent West, life has been comfortable. But we never had any right to be complacent. We have had too many people with preventable diseases, and access to care has been uneven and inequitable. We're unacceptably wasteful on all fronts and we are clearly putting at risk the resilience of our nations and, ultimately, our planet. This is not only about creating happier, healthier families and societies. This is about the health and survival of our entire ecosystem, our entire world.

The good news is that we already have everything we need to respond to today's challenges.

In the midst of fear and occasional chaos, we have seen many generous acts of kindness. We have seen German hospitals accepting Italian patients and Polish health professionals treating British citizens. We've seen private companies donating protective gear to healthcare workers. We have seen small entrepreneurs react spontaneously to solve problems as they've arisen, setting up neighbourhood community services to help those in need. We have seen governments and investors supporting research and scientists around the globe collaborating to develop tests, treatments and vaccines. In our conversation with Thomas Ogilvie, a management board member at Deutsche Post AG, he called this the "rediscovery of humanity in a mixture of mindfulness and decisiveness".

Innovation has accelerated at a remarkable rate. Luxury perfume and vodka producers have turned their hands to making sanitizing gel. Carmakers and fashion houses have switched to producing masks. We've seen impressive resourcefulness in response to the imminent threat of Covid-19. But it does beg the question of why we can't summon the same energy and creativity when facing an Ebola outbreak, or when we are trying to fight leukaemia or the monstrous global threat of climate breakdown.

As Martina Larkin of the World Economic Forum puts it: "Rather than going back to old economic models that we have seen in the past, this is actually a huge chance to rethink economic models, business models and the way we operate, in a fundamental way."

Alex Manson, global head of Standard Chartered Ventures, is an innovation heavyweight, with a lot of first-hand experience of corporate venture building, exactly the kind of innovation approach we will be proposing in detail later in this book. He foresees big changes in the banking sector as a result of the rethinking triggered by Covid-19.

"In any crisis, there will be a split. There'll be a first group of institutions that will just stop there, reduce the burn rate, cut costs and freeze hiring," he says. "They'll revamp their channels because people will want to be online, as opposed to in the branches, but, basically, they'll try to preserve what's out there. On the other side, there'll be a bunch of banks that will actually go: 'Well, maybe that's an opportunity to completely get rid of certain channels and replace them with new ones. Maybe we shouldn't have any branches at all, and this is a great opportunity to accelerate the process and invest more in our digital channels. Maybe we should be coming up with health, lifestyle and finance-related products, which weren't top-of-mind before, but are becoming very much top-of-mind issues right now.'

"But something has to give, obviously, because investment capacity is scarce, so you need to stop doing something in order to do something else. And that redeployment of resources will happen with a few of the financial institutions, as opposed to the first ones who will retrench and preserve what already exists. Obviously, I'm betting that the second category will become a lot more relevant on the back of this crisis than the first one. The jury is out."

CHAMPIONS FOR THE NEW NORMAL

In this book, we explain how leaders in business and society can recapture the sense of urgency and reinvigorate our companies and institutions. Their response will decide whether they will emerge as champions of the new normal, or just play an also-ran role in an average league.

By reacting positively, they can prepare us to tackle a wide range of global issues, from the aftermath of Covid-19 to the need to create a healthier and more resilient society, the disruption of traditional industries and the ultimate challenge posed by climate change.

The new normal will be driven by changing values. Financial outcomes are easy-to-measure proxy indicators for success, but they don't recognize the importance of public goods, such as the environment. In the light of the 2020 pandemic, societies will long for more resilience and agility, leading to the emergence of new markets in areas that relate to the UN's Sustainable Development Goals. Companies of all types, in every sector, will have a contribution to make. As they master the new normal, they will also find themselves positioned to address new and profitable markets.

Drivers of change – new normal

Recent history shows us that demanding targets like this cannot be reached with existing approaches and methods. We will need to be far more ambitious in our use of new technologies, like 3D printing, AI, robotics and ubiquitous computing, asset classes such as (corporate) venture capital and corporate venture building and investment activities such as M&A. But none of this will be enough without some radical rethinking of corporate and government structures and a new commitment to collaboration.

Everyone's in favour of collaboration, at least in broad, general terms. How can you be against it? It's like truth and beauty, motherhood and apple pie. But the new model of collaboration – innovative, cross-sectoral, international, goal-focused, demanding – is hard to achieve.

This kind of collaboration is more than a philosophy or a set of benign intentions. It needs commitment, energy and the willingness to invest resources. We have seen heartening examples of it, in its raw form, in the global response to Covid-19. Now we need to develop the structures and methodologies to make it an enduring force for good, a repeatable phenomenon, a tool that will equip us to respond faster and more decisively than ever before to the vital challenges ahead.

The global impact of the pandemic has underlined the fact that we need a new spirit and practice of collaboration around the globe. The biggest problems – above all, climate change – cannot be confronted or contained within national borders. Neither can the creative destruction of traditional industries, the massive disruption of established companies, jobs and economies triggered by the Fourth Industrial Revolution. Today's big, global tech disrupters are almost all American or Chinese, but many long-established organizations and institutions in both China and the US are facing exactly the same agonizing challenges as their European counterparts.

A MANIFESTO FOR CHANGE

Rapid, purposeful, collaborative innovation is needed everywhere, not just to solve specific problems, but also to restore our sense of urgency and harness our will to retake control of our destiny.

The secret of innovation goes beyond the obvious requirements: intelligence, knowledge, talent, resources and energy. We have all those. But we also need a relentless hunger to grow, to create and implement practical solutions. We need the determination to bring the impossible within reach and to improve everyone's lives, even if our own are already pretty good. "No man is an island," the English poet John Donne wrote, four centuries ago. It's even clearer now. No island is an island. No country or continent is an island. We are interconnected. "Never send to know for whom the bell tolls," Donne went on. "It tolls for thee." To build the world we want for ourselves, and the future we want for our children and grandchildren, we need to start fast – right now.

Technology is giving us the toolkit we need to accelerate the digital transformation of our industries and our societies and create profitable, scalable and sustainable answers to our biggest problems. The new models of global cooperation and collaboration we have glimpsed in the world's response to Covid-19 need to be recognized and exploited for the good of all.

This book is about bringing those elements together. It's about a change of culture and practice that needs to happen very quickly – in this decade. The clock is ticking.

We are not alone in identifying the problem and recognizing that radical solutions are needed. We are standing on the shoulders of giants – the entrepreneurs, business leaders, political leaders, academics and consultants who have seen how current approaches to innovation are failing and who have done good work towards developing new frameworks, methods and tools that address key parts of the jigsaw. We have combined the best of their ideas with our own thinking, research and hands-on experience to leverage existing assets through digital business models. Through corporate venture building, the new asset class will enable governments, corporations, entrepreneurs, doctors, scientists and activists to work together to achieve things that would have seemed impossible years, or even months, ago.

The coronavirus catastrophe has given our world an awful warning of what is to come if we don't change our ways, or change them fast enough. We know now that cooperation – across international borders, across academic disciplines, across industry boundaries – is the only practical way to mobilize our resources in time and at scale. In the next few chapters, we will describe and explain a fresh approach to starting, developing and sustaining the new digital business models that are the key to tackling the next big challenges for the good of companies, economies and populations everywhere.

Section 1 of this book will start by making the case that nothing is an island: our systems have become increasingly interdependent. It will also highlight that, while we know many of the problems that lie ahead of us, especially in healthcare and climate, we're under-utilizing existing assets that could help us meet these complex challenges.

Section 2 will go on to explore the changing rules of tech-enabled business and provide food for thought for business leaders about how they can adapt their strategies to the logic of the new world order.

Section 3 dives deeper into the problems and opportunities of engaging in business to tackle healthcare and climate issues, arguing that we need a new sense of urgency and concerted efforts to protect our wellbeing and that of our planet.

Then, in Section 4, we progress towards the question of solutions, first by looking at the individual level. We will discuss the ingredients required to successfully create new digital value and illustrate the frequent cultural and mindset differences that can get in the way.

Section 5 describes the heart of our own work, defining and explaining corporate venture building as a powerful new asset class that can leverage existing assets through digital business models, with a new incentive system to create value for society.

We'll conclude with a global perspective, arguing that the new normal is not about us versus them, but about a new reality that requires us to work together. And for the last words on the subject, we'll hand the microphone to the future Masters of the New Normal. Section 6 is a call to action from future global leaders who represent more than 50% of the world's population – its young people.

It is quite possible to read each of these sections individually, but we hope you'll enjoy going on the whole journey with us, throughout the book. As you'll quickly recognize, we're entrepreneurs, and we're hardwired to see opportunities in every problem. So we're here to encourage you, the reader, to help us build momentum and create the new normal.

Covid-19 has shown us the faults in our systems. Let's use this impulse to create a better world for ourselves and for the generations to come.

> ● **RULES FOR THE NEW NORMAL**
>
> The cards are being reshuffled. We're realizing how interdependent we are and our rules of engagement are being rewritten by the deep social impact of Covid-19. Those who adapt the fastest can seize tremendous opportunities for society and their organizations. But success requires a new investment approach and different tools.

OUR KEY RECOMMENDATIONS FOR YOU:

- In times of crisis, many leaders instinctively put their companies into survival mode, cutting investment in new business to minimize risk. We think this is dangerous. Our reality is changing fast, and companies need to invest now to meet emerging consumer needs and stay competitive.

- Covid-19 has underlined the point. Tragic as the coronavirus pandemic is, it is only the herald, sent ahead to warn us of more overwhelming disasters. But it has made it painfully clear that inertia is something we can no longer afford. Now is the time to start forging the tools that will make both society and our planet more resilient.

- People talk a lot about what will be different after the virus. But it's just as important, as you define your new strategy, to ask: "What market needs will stay the same?" In many areas – like telemedicine, online working and healthcare data standards – change was already occurring. The pandemic has just been a catalyst, speeding up the rate at which it happened.

- To tackle tomorrow's environmental, health and social challenges, society will need new tools, such as corporate venture building, our preferred approach to creating digital businesses. It will also need a new entrepreneurial mindset, leveraging technology so we can balance supply and demand, green the economy and improve people's health.

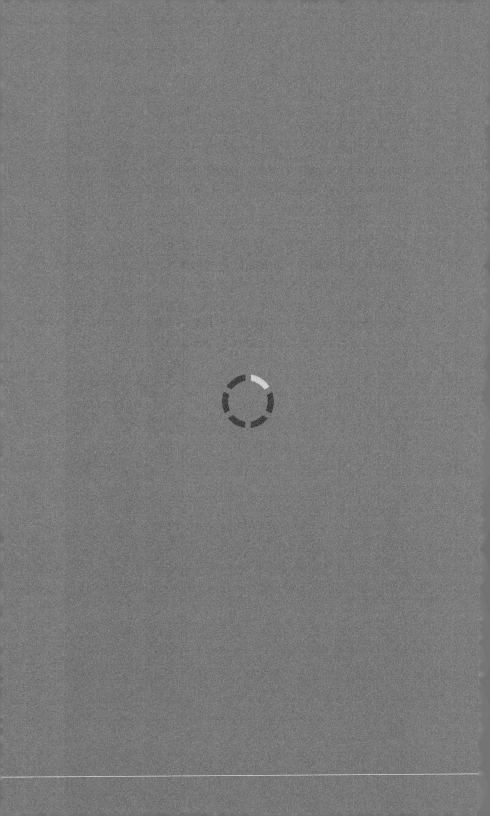

SECTION 1

THE FOURTH INDUSTRIAL REVOLUTION ADDRESSES THE BIG CHALLENGES

NOWHERE IS AN ISLAND

If there's one thing Covid-19 has already taught us, it's that health issues and the economy are inseparably linked. In fact, it has shown us how interdependent everything really is. Covid-19 has only been a sneak peek into the bigger crises that are coming our way. Climate change will be even scarier. But don't worry – we'll get there.

It'll take a coordinated and sustained global response, making full use of all the technologies and talents we have at our disposal, from every country and every industry. It'll require levels of collaboration we have never seen before, drawing on the new structures and new approaches to innovation and investment described in this book. It'll call for an effort of will and a shared determination to look the new reality in the eye and prioritize what really matters most to all of us on this fragile planet.

We are starting from a historic low point, of course. Alongside the terrible health impacts, Covid-19 saw countries incur massive debts that will be with us for decades. Confidence was shattered and jobs and companies were lost. In two months from late February 2020, Britain's FTSE fell 22%, the French CAC 40 was down 25%, Germany's DAX lost 16% and the Dow Jones index was 16% off. Business ground to a halt and hopes of a V-shaped recovery quickly faded. The dawning realization that the major economies were facing months, if not years, of serious disruption was accompanied by warnings of a second wave of infection. At the same time, doctors and scientists began to point out that this stealthy and highly contagious virus was not the only pathogen that could potentially produce such a devastating global catastrophe.

Some experts have even claimed that global warming's melting of the Arctic ice could unleash cryogenically preserved 'zombie viruses', including smallpox, supposedly eradicated since 1977. So far, the traces of smallpox and the deadly 1918 Spanish flu virus discovered in the thawing permafrost have been confirmed as non-viable. But a 2016 outbreak of anthrax, triggered by decades-old bacteria released from the ice of the Siberian tundra, put 20 people in hospital and led to the death of a 12-year-old boy.

If the unlocking of nature's fridge could leave us vulnerable to these and other killer diseases to which humans have no acquired immunity, we may have more to fear from climate breakdown than the obvious dangers of flooding, food shortages and the mass migration of desperate populations. The range of global risks we face is ominous and varied and, as the following illustration shows, they all tend to be connected.

Tackling these risks requires us to make systemic changes through a multi-stakeholder approach

Top 10 global risks

ADAPTED FROM WORLD HEALTH ORGANIZATION

But if there's now a much clearer understanding of the interrelated and interdependent nature of economic, business, climate and health challenges – and of the genuinely global impacts they are likely to have – what kind of organizations and structures are we going to need in the next few years?

Nobody has all the answers. But some of the qualities and characteristics that will be required have suddenly become much clearer.

We will need business and social structures that can support and encourage bold, rapid innovation. We will need them to be open, adaptive and collaborative, respecting the interests and harnessing the strengths and assets of a wide range of stakeholders. We will need them to operate from an international world view and a cross-industry perspective, breaking free from past habits and siloed thinking. And we will need them to have a sense of purpose – however it is defined – that goes beyond merely financial goals.

The young and aggressive tech companies that have replaced the old industrial and petrochemical giants as top dogs in the world economy over the last five years – firms like Apple, Alphabet (Google's holding company), Microsoft, Amazon, Facebook and Alibaba – are all children of the digital revolution. They have grown and diversified fast, generating immense revenues by exploiting digital technology to power platform-based business models that have enabled them to combine and deploy assets and services without the costs and obligations of ownership. This is the beauty of being asset-light and creating value primarily through digital layers – and it's something even the largest corporates can achieve, through adopting the corporate venture building approach.

Platform index

ADAPTED FROM PLATFORM-INDEX.COM

We will come back and look in detail at how Amazon and its peers have gone about achieving their spectacular growth in Section 2. For now, it is enough to recognize that they are all similar in one respect. They have grasped the opportunities for leverage presented by an interconnected world that has thrown open its markets to this kind of commerce without, as yet, developing sophisticated methods of regulating and taxing it.

In the Wild West days of the early stages of digital disruption, they were able to make hay while the sun shone. Their motto was Facebook founder Mark Zuckerberg's combative slogan, quietly dropped in 2014: "Move fast and break things." This buccaneering policy of doing first and asking permission, negotiating compromises or paying fines afterwards has since been adopted with some success by a later generation of fast-growing digital disrupters, including Uber and Airbnb. But it can provoke resistance and retaliation from governments and other institutions. In very heavily regulated sectors like healthcare and pharmaceuticals, confrontation is counterproductive, and it has quickly become apparent that cooperative collaboration offers the only realistic route to swift market penetration.

This is particularly relevant in the area of healthcare. As our graphic shows, there are four major barriers to entry facing any new venture, all of which serve to make rapid scaling difficult.

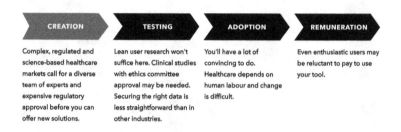

CREATION	TESTING	ADOPTION	REMUNERATION
Complex, regulated and science-based healthcare markets call for a diverse team of experts and expensive regulatory approval before you can offer new solutions.	Lean user research won't suffice here. Clinical studies with ethics committee approval may be needed. Securing the right data is less straightforward than in other industries.	You'll have a lot of convincing to do. Healthcare depends on human labour and change is difficult.	Even enthusiastic users may be reluctant to pay to use your tool.

**Health innovation comes with four limiting steps
that can pose barriers to new ventures**

MORE INFORMATION ON WWW.JOINFIGHTBACK.COM

Collaboration is the only pragmatic strategy, and many companies are realizing that it brings with it many other advantages, over and above the ability to hurdle regulatory and other barriers. This is an important change of emphasis. Health services around the world have yet to reap the benefits of innovative thinking in relation to digital technology. They desperately need what experienced tech entrepreneurs can bring to the table – cutting-edge digital know-how, fast innovation and scale-up techniques, and the kind of uninhibited magpie thinking that recognizes how ideas developed in one sector can be adapted and exploited in a different context. But they are, by their nature, cautious and conservative, rightly protective of the patients and public that depend on them, and understandably risk-averse.

"Obviously this is a very, very tough time.
But that's what entrepreneurs are made of.
They're not made of good times and laziness.
They're made of hard times — that's what life
brings and you take."

PLAMEN RUSSEV
FOUNDER AND CHAIRMAN
OF WEBIT.FOUNDATION

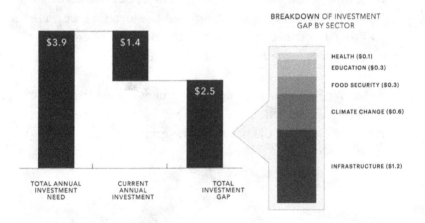

BREAKDOWN OF INVESTMENT
GAP BY SECTOR

$3.9 — TOTAL ANNUAL INVESTMENT NEED
$1.4 — CURRENT ANNUAL INVESTMENT
$2.5 — TOTAL INVESTMENT GAP

HEALTH ($0.1)
EDUCATION ($0.3)
FOOD SECURITY ($0.3)
CLIMATE CHANGE ($0.6)
INFRASTRUCTURE ($1.2)

Sustainable Development Goal sectors need $trillions more

Somehow, structures need to be put in place that enable these established healthcare systems and the corporations that supply them with medicines and services to work closely and productively with the boisterous newcomers to accelerate our responses to the major health and climate change problems of our times.

It can be done. We have seen the future, and it works. We know, from our own direct experience, how this kind of collaborative engagement can be fostered. Much of the rest of this book will be about what we have learned, the mistakes to avoid and how to do it right. But first, we need to take a closer look at the realities of the digitally enhanced post-Covid world we find ourselves in. To get a better view of what's going on, let's zoom out for a moment.

THE REVOLUTION IS WITH US NOW

In 2016, at their annual meeting in Davos, our friends at the World Economic Forum put forward the idea that we were entering a new social, economic and political phase in our global history – the Fourth Industrial Revolution.

As the WEF described it, the development of the world we've known could be seen as a succession of industrial revolutions, each one changing the nature of the game for ever.

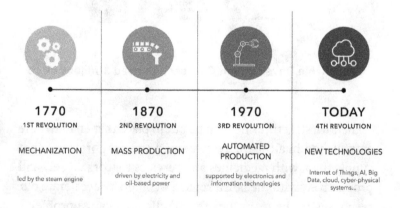

1770	1870	1970	TODAY
1ST REVOLUTION	2ND REVOLUTION	3RD REVOLUTION	4TH REVOLUTION
MECHANIZATION	MASS PRODUCTION	AUTOMATED PRODUCTION	NEW TECHNOLOGIES
led by the steam engine	driven by electricity and oil-based power	supported by electronics and information technologies	Internet of Things, AI, Big Data, cloud, cyber-physical systems...

Four industrial revolutions

The First Industrial Revolution is what was always taught in schools as The Industrial Revolution. It brought deep shaft coal mines and steam-powered machinery, cotton mills and iron foundries, mass transport, in the form of railways, and communications, in the shape of the telegraph network.

The Second Industrial Revolution, in the late 19th and early 20th centuries, brought gas lighting and electric power, steamships and motor vehicles, the telephone and the radio, mass production and assembly lines and, fatally, barbed wire, machine guns and tanks.

The Third Industrial Revolution was all about the coming of computers – first mainframes using punched cards or magnetic tapes that whirred in chilled, air-conditioned shrines, then smaller, increasingly powerful PCs. Computer-aided design, computer-controlled automated machines and computerized records and databases changed the world again, in ways we take for granted so much that we have almost forgotten what things used to be like.

The Fourth Industrial Revolution, triggered by the internet and the smartphone, is still in its early stages. But we can already identify some of the elements that are going to converge to make it another giant step-change. These include new technologies in the fields of artificial intelligence, robotics and cloud computing, blockchain, nanotechnology, materials science and 3D printing, genetics, remote health sensing and biotechnology. As these new capabilities come together, with the digital, the physical and the biological blending in combinations never before imagined, it will change our world. We will see smart factories, smart cities, smart farms, smart homes, smart cars and smart prosthetics, including artificial limbs that move like a human hand or leg.

From now on, everything will be increasingly connected. The Internet of Things is becoming a reality, not just as a way of ensuring your refrigerator never runs out of yoghurt, but as the basis for connected, coordinated, on-demand services that will transform our daily lives and our global business environment. It sounds good, of course. But, as you'll hear from Brigitte Mohn and Marcus Wallenberg in the case studies at the end of this section, change can still be difficult.

In the past, though, companies, governments and individuals operated almost entirely on historical information. Today, we have a wealth of real-time data we can put alongside it. And that changes everything.

"Moving from historical decision-making to real-time decision-making is a huge shift," says Mark Spelman, the World Economic Forum's Head of Thought Leadership. "We can automate decisions and use AI to optimize and improve efficiency."

In many cases, where the flow of information is simply too fast and too complex for the brain to handle, we will be able to utilize this real-time data via instantly responsive AI and machine-learning systems that can outperform any human operator.

For example, one problem for those designing self-driving cars has always been the need for the control systems to be situated on board the vehicle. Even the brief latency periods involved meant that cloud-based control systems couldn't react fast enough to sudden emergencies on the road. But new 5G networks offer latency of 1 to 2 milliseconds, compared with 4G's 50 milliseconds, and that makes all the difference when it comes to avoiding a pothole – or a child. Computing power, and the batteries to run it, must no longer be carried in the car. Or in the delivery drone. Or in each of a hundred autonomous robots in an automated factory.

Transport, logistics and manufacturing are likely to provide many of the most striking examples of the coming digital transformation. But there are other important domains where revolutionary change is afoot. Healthcare is one key area where the devastating impact of Covid-19 has undoubtedly speeded up the pace of change. It provides a classic example of how you need to think through the full implications of these developments in a specific industry.

FROM INTUITION TO PRECISION MEDICINE

As far as healthcare is concerned, the First and Second Industrial Revolutions can be seen as a single era: the age of intuitive medicine. The period from the beginning of the 19th century to the early part of the 20th saw the abandonment of many superstitions and erroneous beliefs, such as the long-cherished miasma theory, which held that most fatal diseases were spread by bad odours, or even just by 'night air'.

Science began to make its mark with the introduction of ideas like vaccination and anaesthetics, painkillers such as morphine and aspirin, the antiseptic treatment of wounds, and vital public health measures like the pasteurization of milk and the provision of safe water supplies. But medicine still depended on the identification of symptoms, and many symptoms – like fever, coughing, diarrhoea and vomiting, and headaches – were associated with any number of different disorders. Diseases were hard to tell apart. 'Consumption', for example, was recognized as a major cause of death. But the wasting, pain and breathing difficulties that were labelled 'consumption' could be caused by anything from tuberculosis to lung cancer. Doctors looked for patterns of symptoms that they recognized and went with their gut feelings and experience. Medicine was ultimately intuitive.

During the period of the Third Industrial Revolution, doctors, aided by new technologies that allowed them to accumulate and process vast amounts of data, were able to identify diseases more accurately and measure the effectiveness of different treatments. Powerful new drugs, such as antibiotics, antivirals, corticosteroids, paracetamol and ibuprofen were added to the armoury, alongside new interventions like chemo and radiotherapy, and medicine became the empirical, evidence-based discipline we are all familiar with.

Even with all the medical advances of the last 60 or 70 years, though, we still tend to treat patients with reference to their symptoms, rather than the specific causes of their conditions. The new medical technologies associated with the Fourth Industrial Revolution are changing this and moving us into a new era: the age of precision medicine. It is now recognized that precise, specific diagnosis is the key to developing and tailoring predictably effective treatment for every patient. Better data and tech breakthroughs, such as molecular diagnostics and genetic testing and better imaging, serology and point-of-care diagnostic techniques are already helping doctors target their therapies and treatments in ways that would not have been possible just a few years ago.

But raising healthcare standards is not just a matter of developing better drugs and treatment methods. Countries have widely differing approaches to health provision, ranging from universal healthcare systems, paid for through taxation and free at the point of use, like Britain's NHS or Italy's SSN, to public insurance-based universal schemes (like China, Japan and France), universal hybrid public/private insurance systems (like Germany and Turkey), universal private insurance systems (like Switzerland) or non-universal insurance systems (like the US, India and Egypt), which can potentially leave the poor with no access at all to medical services. However healthcare is funded, rising expectations and ageing populations inexorably lead to increased demand, even without the potentially overwhelming shock of a pandemic like Covid-19.

Every health system needs to explore new ways of delivering its services and expanding its scope within the limitations of its budget. There is never enough cash to do everything that needs to be done, but there are a number of ways advances in digital technology can help to make healthcare more efficient. For example, by using real-time information, alongside historical data, it should be possible to allocate resources, including medicines and supplies of protective equipment, much more quickly and efficiently and to spot and track outbreaks of infectious diseases as soon as they start to develop.

More importantly, primary care physicians who have been forced to use remote triage (deciding which patients need priority treatment) and smartphone video consultations during the Covid-19 crisis have discovered that their patients don't always need face-to-face appointments. They often want advice or reassurance, rather than a visit to the doctor, and a brief online chat now may be a welcome alternative to waiting days or weeks for an appointment, or risking infection by going to a surgery or hospital.

The next step on from this may be a greater role for telemedicine, which is already providing first-line medical services for enormous numbers of patients around the world. In China,

Ping An's Good Doctor telemedicine service claims more than 300 million users, and its rivals, including JD Health, Tencent's WeDoctor and Alibaba's Ali Health, have all attracted millions of new users in the wake of the coronavirus disaster.

As Jonathan Larsen of Ping An points out: "There are many factors that will continue to drive costs and create challenges. Many people think that the only way China can solve these problems is through breakthrough models and creative applications of new technology."

TELEMEDICINE REACHES OUT TO MORE PATIENTS

Telemedicine has the potential to allow doctors to make better use of their time, see more people, get a second opinion quickly and easily, monitor their patients' conditions (everything from lung function and blood pressure to glucose levels), provide routine reviews and advice for those with chronic ailments, avoid the risk of becoming infected themselves and even continue working if they have to be quarantined.

Patients who live far away or are too ill to travel can avoid unnecessary journeys. Well organized telemedicine systems can give the sick on-demand access to acute care, including out-of-hours services, eliminate missed appointments and lower the cost of providing diagnosis and treatment for many common conditions.

All these factors may yield important benefits in countries with advanced economies. In less developed societies, they offer the opportunity to reduce health inequalities and extend quality care to large urban and rural populations that currently have unfulfilled needs. The Medical Council of India, for example, has recently stated, partly in response to the Covid-19 emergency, that telemedicine should be used to minimize barriers to access and that it is seen as "a critical enabler for the overall transformation of the health system".

Telemedicine, as we know it today, is not a magic wand. In fact, one reason for its surprisingly slow take-up in many countries may be that early enthusiasts oversold its revolutionary potential and frightened off those who could use it in modest, practical and unspectacular ways. As one young doctor told us recently: "Telemedicine's just a treatment delivery mechanism that can be utilized – with some patients, some of the time – to provide high-quality care."

But all this is just first-generation stuff, mostly aimed at amplifying the effectiveness of today's medical professionals. In China, they are already embarking on the next steps. Starting in 2018, Ping An Good Doctor has installed hundreds of unmanned AI-powered self-service healthcare kiosks in airports and stations, shopping malls, pharmacies and university campuses.

Good Doctor's customers sit in a tiny cabin, like an automated photo booth equipped with a range of smart medical examination devices, and respond to questions about their symptoms. They are hooked up to a vast AI knowledge bank with details of 3,000 diseases, which delivers a diagnosis – or a recommendation for further investigation – almost instantly. These little kiosks, known as One-Minute Clinics, have proved wildly popular and are being rolled out across the country.

In the hospital context, too, the revolution is starting to make itself felt in futuristic ways. Remote robotic surgery is slowly becoming more practical, aided by 5G's lightning fast response times. (The first showpiece demonstration, known as the Lindbergh Operation, was back in 2001 and involved a surgeon in New York removing the gallbladder of a woman 6,000 km away in France.) Tele-ICU allows one centrally-located specialist to guide the actions of several intensive care teams in remote locations. And deep learning algorithms can already match or exceed the performance of clinical specialists when it comes to distinguishing melanomas from benign skin lesions, or detecting the early signs of certain types of breast cancer. Disease by disease, digital technology is helping us make the finer distinctions that enable us to unpack the different conditions that have historically been lumped together under catch-all labels like lung cancer, hypertension, asthma and Type 2 diabetes.

These are clearly significant advances, but they raise ethical problems, too. In particular, the question of whether AI and machine learning systems should ever be allowed to specify treatments and medication, without the direct supervision of experienced doctors, is a complicated and nuanced issue that is likely to be determined as much by cultural factors as by any assessments of medical efficacy.

Players both in and outside the health system are gradually learning to navigate the complexities, add to the range of services remote healthcare can offer and get patients more involved in managing their own health issues. Doktor24 (a corporate venture building project) and Ada Health (a non-corporate start-up) are two interesting case studies that illustrate how this is already being done.

COVID'S GOT US THINKING DIFFERENTLY

In a matter of weeks, Covid-19 showed us a world we had never experienced before. Urban centres were deserted. Shops and businesses were shuttered. There were more bicycles than cars on the roads and more walkers than cyclists. The skies were empty and birdsong was everywhere.

In the sleepy Welsh resort of Llandudno, a herd of long-horned Kashmiri goats came down from the nearby mountain and took over the town. Leopards were seen in the streets of Mumbai and Islamabad, kangaroos in Melbourne and jackals in central Johannesburg. People in rural India peeped from their windows as herds of elephants rumbled slowly through their villages.

Millions of office workers discovered that going in every day was not necessarily an essential part of their job. Dressing from the waist up, they sat at their desks or tables at home and took part in remote meetings powered by Zoom, FaceTime, Google Meet, Skype, WhatsApp and similar video technologies. Many face-to-face meetings began to seem like an expensive and wasteful luxury. Internationally, entry restrictions meant that the endless round of business travel came to an abrupt halt.

Greenhouse gas emissions plummeted and satellite images showed dramatic falls in air pollution.

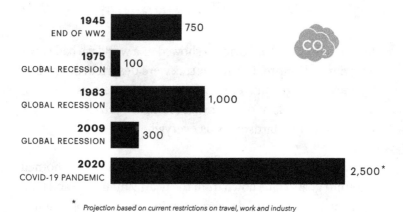

1945
END OF WW2 — 750

1975
GLOBAL RECESSION — 100

1983
GLOBAL RECESSION — 1,000

2009
GLOBAL RECESSION — 300

2020
COVID-19 PANDEMIC — 2,500*

CO₂

* *Projection based on current restrictions on travel, work and industry*

Covid-19 could cause 2.5 billion ton drop in CO$_2$ emissions

ADAPTED FROM STATISTA, 2020

Optimists began to dream of a sudden lunge forward in our attempts to fend off the global disaster of climate breakdown. They saw the recovery from the pandemic as a spectacular one-off opportunity to move away from fossil fuels and accelerate the switch to cleaner energy. Governments, they said, could make bailouts and economic stimulus and business support programmes conditional on cutting emissions, reducing fossil fuel consumption and investing in wind and solar power.

Pessimists pointed to the widespread assumption that things would soon be back to normal, and to the postponement of November's UN climate change summit, at which more than 190 countries were due to reveal their updated plans to meet the legally binding emission reduction targets established under 2015's Paris Agreement. They worried about the US government's relaxation of environmental protection and auto emissions laws, about China's extended deadlines for environmental compliance and about Brazil's announcement that it would ease controls on logging in the Amazon rain-forest. In Europe, they were troubled by Poland's withdrawal of support for a planned carbon trading programme and the Czech Republic's call for the EU to abandon its new European Climate Law proposals, aimed at forcing the continent to become climate-neutral by 2050.

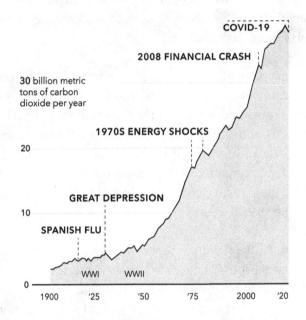

Large falls after global crises have been followed by sharp increases in emissions

ADAPTED FROM GLOBAL CARBON PROJECT

Despite the opposition, though, the EU is not backing off.

"While our immediate focus is on combating Covid-19, our work on delivering the European Green Deal continues," a spokesman said in April 2020. "The climate crisis is still a reality and necessitates our continued attention and effort."

Some influential people, like Martina Larkin of the World Economic Forum, even see it as an opportunity to drive forward the green agenda. She's a realist, though. "It cannot come at the cost of those who are left behind," she says. "It has to be a green recovery that's also inclusive."

Political will, however, is not going to be enough. Capitalist, consumerist societies advance through the choices and actions of businesses and consumers.

The widespread adoption of mobile phones – to the point where, after less than 20 years, the world now has more internet-connected smartphones than toilets – underlines the fact that affordable, useful technologies change people's lives quickly and forever. If we are to save the planet from the disaster of climate change, we must make it possible and attractive for people to choose products and services that will move us in that direction.

Politicians in democratic countries can use the levers they have at their disposal, adjusting taxes and incentives, exhorting and cajoling businesses and individuals to redirect their investments and change their habits. But they can't change the world by diktat – and they can't do it alone.

The only way climate breakdown can be averted is through partnership and collaboration, between governments and businesses, NGOs and entrepreneurs, popular movements and individual consumers. We need new structures, new ways of working together, new technologies to make this easier and a new determination to safeguard our people and our world. Our best hope lies in the tools the Fourth Industrial Revolution has already given us and the new ones that will emerge over the next few years.

Mark Spelman of the World Economic Forum sees exciting new possibilities emerging that we could not have dreamt of even a few years ago. The Fourth Industrial Revolution could be our saviour, if we succeed in harnessing its full potential.

"Taken together, connectivity, real-time information and these new combinations of new technologies are fundamentally a decentralizing force," he says. "This basically puts power into the hands of the consumer and the citizen."

To unleash this power, however, we need our entrepreneurs (people like Anna Alex of Planetly, featured in our case study at the end of this section) and our engineers, managers and policymakers to act with purpose, and in alignment, to put our collective intellectual and technological power into effect. Or, to put it more bluntly: if we don't all get off our bottoms and start collaborating intensely, our species is pretty much finished.

But when we mobilize these forces, we must be clear about which opportunities we want to pursue.

As Michael G. Jacobides of the London Business School and his co-author Martin Reeves point out: "Deciding which ones to back requires both carefully observing emerging actual trends and distinguishing between temporary and more permanent shifts in demand.

"Many of the immediately observed shifts in response to Covid-19 were driven by either fear of infection or compliance with official directives, and were therefore likely to be temporary. But others were accompanied by increased convenience or better economics, so they were more likely to stick."

As we face the future, we will need to create the right incentives to drive the structural shifts that will enable us to take better care of ourselves and our environment. But before we discuss how we can amalgamate our inventive forces to pre-empt the next disaster, it will be useful to dive a little deeper into the details of the changing business environment and the challenges we're facing, so you'll see the connections before we come to describing our solution.

KEY CONCEPTS

1. **WE'RE ALL IN THIS TOGETHER**
   The 2020s have already taught us how interdependent we all are, especially in relation to climate and health challenges. But we're also coming to understand that key solutions can be found through creative collaboration.

2. **THE LOW-HANGING FRUIT HAS ALREADY GONE**
   The Fourth Industrial Revolution's quick wins are running out. To stay relevant and tackle society's biggest and most intractable problems, we must drastically change the way we create new businesses.

3. **INNOVATION LIMBO**
   While most wealthy societies have powerful assets they could leverage to solve these emerging problems, they have not been good at exploiting their potential.

OUR KEY RECOMMENDATIONS FOR YOU:

- Our global system is increasingly interdependent, and the speed of change is faster than ever. In the fog of uncertainty, we need more trustworthy data, in manageable, standardized formats. Platform business models are important, as they can help match supply and demand where it is needed most.

- It's the complexity of today's global challenges that makes them so hard to tackle. Every large corporation has many assets (plant, data, experienced talent and so on) that you can potentially unleash in the digital space, using new approaches like corporate venture building.

- We believe a range of profitable markets are still untapped because of high barriers to entry. Many of these offer major opportunities to improve our own health (e.g. through value-based healthcare and precision medicine) and that of the environment (e.g. through technology-enabled sharing).

- The good news is that we have what it takes to make these things happen. We have the data, historic and new. We have the technology. And we have the infrastructure needed to implement truly groundbreaking ideas.

- It's not just up to creative start-ups like Planetly or Doktor24 and their investors to drive this kind of change. Other players in the ecosystem, including governments, have a major role to play. We should create opportunities in areas where innovation can benefit society.

- Incentive structures in every field encourage people – from politicians and C-level business leaders to front-line work-ers – to focus on short-term goals. They are incentivized to aim for quarterly or year-on-year impact, or to measure success in the years between elections. This must change.

TOP-DOWN, BOTTOM-UP – SEEING CHANGE FROM BOTH SIDES

Dr Brigitte Mohn knows what it takes to spark a revolution. She sees that Europe has all the ingredients to be a global leader in digitization and is wasting no time to help get it there as fast as possible. She does this in her roles as a member of the Executive Board at Bertelsmann Stiftung (the Bertelsmann Foundation), Chair of the Board of Trustees at the German Stroke Foundation, and a shareholder in Bertelsmann Verwaltungsgesellschaft. Proactive and forward-looking, she drives innovation on a daily basis, championing both corporate responsibility and social entrepreneurship.

Bertelsmann, founded in 1835, originally specialized in theological literature. Today, it is the majority shareholder of the RTL Group, with 75% of the shares. RTL operates more than 60 television stations, 30 radio stations and eight video-on-demand platforms. Bertelsmann also owns 75% of Penguin Random House, the world's largest trade book publisher, with 275 imprints and brands on six continents, and vast interests in music, magazines, business services and education businesses. Brigitte represents the sixth generation of the Mohn family on the supervisory board of this multinational corporation.

Her main job is her work on the management board of Bertelsmann Stiftung, founded by her father, Reinhard Mohn, in 1977, and dedicated to the idea that competition and civic engagement are the basis of social progress. As a private foundation, it runs a wide range of projects aimed at addressing the challenges of the digitized, globalized future in a positive way.

Since promoting entrepreneurship and social innovations are among her most important personal motives, she supports start-ups in a private capacity.

So she has a unique perspective, taking in the view from the heights of a huge, long-established corporation, her management experience with the foundation and the down-to-earth struggles of new start-ups.

When we asked her about the threats and opportunities created by digital technology, new business models and the Fourth Industrial Revolution, we found she has strong views about Europe's slow response to today's fast-changing business environment.

"There are three factors holding us back," she explains. "In my view, companies do not yet see the full potential of digitization clearly enough. This is the risk of over-estimating one's own competitiveness in increasingly globalized markets. Many companies just think they're already good enough to compete. They haven't under-stood the real risks yet.

"Then there is a concern about change, which certainly affects people's behaviour. I see a lack of trying new approaches, perhaps combined with the worry of having to accept early setbacks – 'If I do that and fail, what happens then?' We in Europe need to take a look at what innova-tors in other countries are doing. And I think we could do more to encourage curiosity and inventiveness much more strongly at an early age in our educational institutions."

In addition to cultural constraints, she believes, another part of the challenge is that there is no agreement about what Europe should be achieving in terms of growth. This lack of clarity in the political sphere has implications for the way industry responds to the transformation process.

"It is important to become solution-oriented, which is going to involve building platform-based companies and a network of ecosystems," she says. "Investments in technologies such as artificial intelligence are also crucial, and there are many opportunities."

Europe's big corporations obviously need to explore more ways to inject innovative technology and entrepreneurial flair into their systems and attitudes. Conventional approaches to R&D are unlikely to deliver radically new solutions and innovations fast enough to provide the answers that are needed, and it is equally important to create legal frameworks that promote innovation.

Some of the new initiatives that have emerged over the last few years, like the corporate venture building model, have already demonstrated how this can be done. Mohn sees a first reaction by Europe to the fast-moving, disruptive competitors from America and China beginning to show through in a more positive determination to adopt the methods that work best in today's digital environment.

"We'll need new forms of cooperation, new partnerships and joint ventures and a new dialogue between politics and business," she says, "if we're going to make this a winning story."

DOKTOR24'S IRON MAN HAS THE PRESCRIPTION FOR GROWTH

Iron Man may be a fictional character, but he has real-life competition in the shape of Alexander Wennergren Helm of Doktor24. A passionate Ironman triathlete and an entrepreneurial business leader, Wennergren Helm is creating a healthier life through innovation across the Nordic countries and around the globe. As in sport, he's mastered multiple disciplines in business. He has grown large and powerful organizations as CEO of healthcare provider Aleris and at Hultafors Group, which makes construction equipment. And he's also co-founded and scaled up young and innovative tech start-ups like Doktor24, where he's Chairman of the Board.

Doktor24 has just announced, as one of the first suppliers in the world, that it is now able to provide Covid-19 antibody tests all over Sweden. The firm, which has 80 employees, is a disruptive digital care specialist, founded by Aleris but now an independent company, which provides healthcare and radiology services across Scandinavia, with the aim of realizing the potential of digitalized healthcare.

To make healthcare more accessible and convenient, Doktor24 automates many crucial processes in the patient care path, facilitates communication between patients and healthcare providers, enables payments and helps with patient management.

Doktor24 started as Aleris X, a digital venture founded by Aleris, whose specialist care operations cover hospitals, outpatient clinics and radiology units in more than 100 locations, performing a million X-rays every year.

The Aleris X team started out with a broad mandate to explore opportunities to digitize healthcare, with no pre-ordained strategic restrictions. It soon started to discover formidable opportunities in the market by adopting an 'outside-in' perspective, rather than an Aleris perspective.

"The young spin-off went off on a different type of evolution from what we expected and, as time went by, the company became more and more independent from the mother ship," Wennergren Helm told us. "The companies grew apart, and Aleris X developed into Doktor24, an independent care provider and technology supplier, with Aleris as a customer for its services.

"In the end, we built something that was not as valuable as Aleris itself, but was really valuable to society. We are making healthcare more available and more productive. We are utilizing resources in a less wasteful manner and are more inclusive towards patients."

Wennergren Helm believes they could not have achieved nearly as much if they had tried to restrain Aleris X or tether it tightly to the parent company. And his advice to fellow corporate leaders launching completely new digital businesses is all the more powerful through being based directly on his own experience.

"Focus on setting the right foundations when you start the process, get the right people on board, set some directions and be clear about how open you need it to be. Then allow it to grow into an independent unit that may become completely separate and different from your original idea.

"Transformative innovation is a search process that takes you into unknown territory," he adds. "If you try to restrict that too much, I'm not sure you're likely to have a good success rate in your innovation. Incremental innovation in the core business has to be done using a tighter process."

FROM THE MORAL SYSTEM TO THE BUSINESS SYSTEM

Anna Alex first made a name for herself as the founder of the personal clothes shopping service Outfittery, creating a successful company in the e-commerce fashion space and winning many accolades – as a member of Europe's 'Inspiring Fifty', as one of the 'Young Elite – Top 40 under 40' and as one of 'the most inspiring women in tech'.

Now she's on a new mission. Driven by the wish to deal with the climate crisis actively and entrepreneurially, she has founded Planetly, with her colleague Benedikt Franke, to bring meaningful transparency to the measuring of carbon emission footprints.

"We need to play the game to win the game," Alex told us. She is hopeful that we will eventually be able to change the system for the better. But she is realistic.

"This will take a while, and we don't have any time when it comes to the climate crisis. The decade of delivery has begun. So our approach is to play the system and understand it, instead of judging. We're happy to support any company that wants to move towards climate neutrality."

Her approach is to find models that balance purpose and profit.

"Impact is purpose plus scale. In order to achieve scale, we decided not to be a non-profit organization, but to have a really solid business model behind us. In our case, it's a SaaS (software as a service) business model, so we will just charge the customer software licensing fees. By taking this route, we are able to attract investors and use the investors' money to make the business big."

Planetly has just raised first-round funding of €5.2 million – a remarkable amount of money for a hard-to-prove business model. Interestingly, the three main funds that Planetly took on board are not typical impact investors or subject-matter focused investors, which must be a good sign for other aspiring climate entrepreneurs.

So what made Planetly so convincing for these willing backers?

"Our vision is to be the most actionable tool to fight the climate crisis," says Alex. "Being 'actionable' is really at the core of what we do. This involves, for example, automating data collection. As long as it's manual and done by consultants who are running through a company with Excel spreadsheets, which was my own experience with my former company, it's not actionable, because it's only done once a year. And if you know your next emissions assessment is only going to be coming along in a year's time, some time next May, you don't change your behaviour. It's not actionable."

Actionable, to Planetly, means automating data collection as much as possible and following up with very practical advice on how to reduce your emissions.

"Then you offset, as well," she says, "and you show the world that you've offset your emissions to encourage others to move in the same direction.

"When it comes to how to communicate this, it is, to a certain extent, translation work — from the moral system to the business system."

OPPORTUNITIES, AS WELL AS THREATS

Marcus Wallenberg, Chair of FAM and Patricia Industries and Vice Chair of Investor AB and the Wallenberg
Foundations, is a fifth-generation member of the
banking and investment family that once, in the early
1990s, indirectly controlled an estimated one-third
of Sweden's GNP. He is a key figure in the country's
business life, as chairman of both Saab and SEB, the
bank founded by his ancestors 164 years ago.

But he is anything but a traditionalist. When we interviewed him for *FightBack*, Wallenberg was eager to
talk about the impact of digitization, new business
models and the urgency with which established
corporations need to respond to the challenges of the
Fourth Industrial Revolution.

"People see the need for change," he told us.
"But they are not spending enough, and they're not
spending it quickly enough. There are huge opportunities out there, but people need to be quick. Every
company, in every sector, faces the threat of significant disruption."

SEB, for example, is a relatively small retail bank.
With just a hundred branches and 4.5 million customers, its operating costs are high, compared with the
costs of running a huge organization like Alibaba's Ant
Financial Services, which is able to spread the costs
of running its payments, loans, credit card and wealth
management businesses across a customer base of
nearly 600 million active digital users.

"Ant Financial will be entering Europe soon," says Wallenberg. "So how do we begin to compete with that? Our family business has lived through the previous three industrial revolutions, but the Fourth Industrial Revolution is creating very dramatic changes for society as a whole and for SEB and all the companies we invest in."

Part of the answer, he believes, is to ensure that private and public sector organizations have access to the tools and technologies that are reshaping our world. The Wallenberg Foundations started investing heavily in AI and quantum computing five years ago and have been deeply involved in Combient, a non-profit cross-industry collaboration network that brings 30 major Scandinavian companies, including KONE, Husqvarna, SAS, Electrolux and Scania, together with technologists, entrepreneurs, start-ups and universities.

Combient is about helping these players pool their talents, energies and resources to co-create new services and products, using emerging technologies and new digital business models. In its first couple of years, it has spawned over 100 innovative solutions, using the buying power of the big companies, in the role of early adopters, to help them gain that first vital foothold in the market.

"We need to focus on satisfying customers' real needs," says Wallenberg. "It's about delivering better, cheaper solutions. We see that in the banking context, with SEB, where the innovative fintechs have shown themselves to be very good at focusing on narrow segments and nibbling away at us.

"But you do see examples, too, in the government sector, where technology creates big opportunities to improve productivity and redirect resources into more useful roles. In the south of Sweden, for instance, they've created a machine-learning robot that's cut the time needed to check social security files, so that claimants get their benefit money in days, rather than weeks, and staff can be freed up to provide practical help to people out in the field, including those who are looking for jobs."

Some of the big Nordic businesses Investor AB and unlisted holding company FAM have stakes in are already radically changing their approach to business, in ways that might seem startling. KONE and Scania (neither of them owned by Investor or FAM) have redefined their roles as being about 'transporting people', rather than making lifts and escalators or trucks and buses. But this is not some blue-sky business school brainstorming exercise. These are companies that each employ some 50,000 people, and rethinking their business models is the first step towards positioning them for major digital-driven transformations.

Wallenberg backs the FightBack manifesto, with its emphasis on the urgent need for new digital business models, collaboration between entrepreneurs, executives, investors and policymakers and the shared mission to create a better future. He is an optimist, though, and he's keen to point out the benefits that digital technologies and new business models can bring.

"There are many opportunities, as well as threats," he says. "We must help people see that new jobs and career chances will emerge to replace those lost through automation.

"We need to explain the positive aspects of digital transformation. We didn't do a good job of explaining and preparing for globalization – and we need to do a lot better when it comes to digitization."

SECTION 2

HYBRID PLATFORMS CAN TAKE
US A LONG WAY, ONCE WE MOVE
BEYOND THE HYPE

BIG QUESTIONS NEED BIG ANSWERS

A journey of a thousand miles begins with a single step, insisted Chairman Mao. He was right, in that making a start is essential to getting things done. In every other respect, he was horribly wrong. Take that first single step and you still have roughly 1,999,999 to go. Setting out to cover a thousand miles one step at a time is not a smart strategy.

When we're faced with problems that flare fast and unpredictably, like the coronavirus crisis, or that are accelerating, taking different forms and threatening our world in many different ways, like global warming, it's clear that pedestrian, step-by-step solutions are never going to give us the answers that will avert disaster. What we need are big, ambitious, innovative, scalable, science-based responses. We need initiatives that can be tried out fast, prove their potential in small, carefully monitored pilots, and then expand exponentially to make a global impact. But we also need thousands of initiatives without global ambitions that focus on solving unique local challenges.

And, up to now, we've not been very good at creating either type of solution.

The industrial and commercial giants of yesteryear have lost their confidence, their dynamism and their sense of purpose – and, with them, their seats at the top table. Even General Electric, a proud member of the Dow Jones Industrial Average for more than a century, dropped out of the index in 2018. It's no coincidence that the young lords of the Earth that have taken over from them – the Amazons, Apples, Microsofts, Alphabets and Alibabas – are all aggressive, digitally-driven, platform-based businesses, with global reach and awesome competitive muscle.

But neither the old guard nor the all-conquering newcomers have the will or the capacity to square up to the world's most urgent and potentially devastating challenges.

If we are to fight back against the existential threats posed by global pandemics and climate breakdown, we are going to need a completely new approach. Our existing models for leveraging technology, as we will see in Section 3, are either too shortsighted or too slow to help us deal with these big and complex problems.

As we spell out in Section 5 of this book, we will need new tools and new collaborative structures and alliances that bring together governments and corporations, universities and entrepreneurs, scientists and doctors, researchers and financiers and NGOs. We will need new ways to exploit their different strengths, mobilize their resources, fire up their inventive and innovative talents and come up with new and unimagined solutions that can be deployed quickly and effectively. As you'll see, the new approach of corporate venture building is the ideal asset class to make this happen.

It won't be easy. But we have the tools we need. We now have access to a vast range of rapidly advancing technologies – artificial intelligence and machine learning, 5G and cloud services, IoT sensing and reporting, blockchain and nanotechnology, robotics and genomics.

If you've come across FoundersLane before, you might expect us, at this point, to share valuable lessons with you about how to orchestrate widely distributed networks of players with different interests, capabilities and concerns, based on our research into the ways Amazon, Alibaba and the rest of them use their platforms to organize and influence the business ecosystems around them.

We could do that. But it isn't simple. There really aren't any one-size-fits-all solutions we could offer you in a few neat paragraphs. And one of the big problems with platform thinking is that it's often based on clichés and half-digested principles. Look closely and you'll find that many famous platform companies are burning their investors' money in unsustainable ways to keep their hold on volatile customers.

As the London Business School's Michael G. Jacobides puts it: "People start with truisms that are not thought through and examples that are not typical."

Not all platforms are created equal – and neither are markets or underlying technologies. For most companies today, we'd probably even advise against building your own platform.

But you're right: this section is very much about how platform business models work.

NO MORE BUSINESS AS USUAL

Most managers in large and long-established organizations have been slow to make the radical changes required to reshape them for the digital age. This is not usually because they don't recognize the need. It is more likely to be because they don't yet understand how digital business models – and especially platform-based models – can be applied to their particular circumstances. They admire and dread the unstoppable growth of the digital leaders, but they don't know how it's done, beyond a vague feeling that it's to do with combining bold innovation methodologies, new business models and cutting-edge digital technologies. And most haven't yet fully understood the existential threats these technological and business model innovations pose for their companies.

After having made their first significant profits through disintermediation (cutting out the middleman), the platform companies are increasingly taking over the entire supply chain of a product or service (they call it 'vertical integration'). Amazon, for one, has long been producing its own products based on the extensive market data it harvests from its users. As these companies go into healthcare, they are already providing their own services, rather than just matching supply and demand. Amazon founder and CEO Jeff Bezos's famous saying, "Your margin is my profit" is becoming even less palatable now.

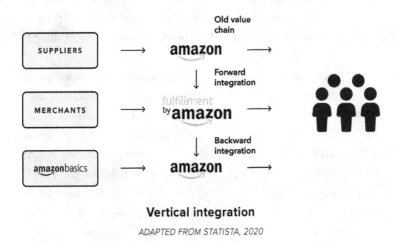

Vertical integration

ADAPTED FROM STATISTA, 2020

There are plenty of signs of activity and concern across almost every industry, and there's a lot of earnest talk about the need for 'digital transformation'. But most of it falls far short of what is needed. Companies that don't really know where they should be heading or what their future markets will look like often indulge in 'innovation theatre', setting up well-meaning initiatives like hackathons, in-house incubator units and accelerator programmes or launching lean start-up and design thinking training schemes. This is often combined with 'innovation tourism' in the shape of trips to Silicon Valley or Shenzhen. But the net result of these efforts is rarely any significant improvement in company performance. And when public sector organizations try the same sort of thing, the outcomes tend to be equally disappointing. Old habits of linear, incremental thinking are just as deeply entrenched in the state sector as they are in the corporate world.

The choices facing established organizations are stark. 'Digitize or decline' is the first, brutal option. But beyond that there is the decision to be made about whether to edge ahead with incremental innovation or embrace new business models and start laying positive foundations for a radically different future.

Every industry under the sun – from banking and manufacturing to healthcare and energy – is busy trying to automate and digitize as many of its processes as possible. The potential gains, in terms of speed, efficiency and reduced costs, are obvious. But the digitization of existing processes is not the big story. It may be necessary, but it is not going to be enough. That's just table stakes, the price you pay to stay alive in the game. Merely doing what you've always done, but doing it faster and more efficiently, will not guarantee future success – or even survival.

We have already seen how new technologies have changed the rules of the game and created unimagined possibilities for new growth and new products and services. But even those managers who recognize that we are in the early stages of the Fourth Industrial Revolution have generally failed to understand how far-reaching the changes will be.

The real revolution lies in the way value is created and captured in the new digital, connected world. We have seen these changes beginning to make their mark over several years, but there is no doubt that the seismic shock of the coronavirus pandemic will concentrate minds and force the pace.

Leaders will have to take big decisions that will shape the future for their businesses. In the wake of Covid-19, they will need to reset both their short-term ambitions and their long-term strategies. They will need to choose whether to try to rebuild and reinstate the customer relationships, supply chains and production facilities they had come to take for granted over the years or to bet on their ability to come up with new ideas, new service and product offerings and new digital business ventures.

They were already having to grapple with the new dynamics of business. Now they are being forced to reset their strategic goals – and that can be a challenging and uncomfortable process. But for those who are prepared to back their own judgement and commit themselves to a future of radical change and innovation, there will be new opportunities, alongside the obvious challenges. We are seeing this already, with a growing number of companies showing a serious interest in using corporate venture building to master new concepts like platform-based business models and ecosystems and harness the new skills and resources needed to capture their potential.

Many are still hesitant, though, uncertain about the risks involved in leaving behind the old ways and the business cultures they grew up in. They have a point. Platforms have acquired an almost mythical status, creating a desire among many leaders to throw a platform business model over everything with an economic pulse. Michael G. Jacobides points to a fallacious assumption he calls the 'LeBron James Illusion', in which people think that because the basketball star shoots well from outside seven metres, they, too, should shoot from outside seven metres to be a successful player. That's simply confusing cause and effect. You are not going to become tall, or LeBron James, just by playing a lot of basketball and shooting from long range.

In fact, building a platform business requires a deep understanding of the way the mechanics work, ample funding, the right assets and timescales, plus some form of legitimacy among the incumbents in the market that you are about to disintermediate. The key strategic question, therefore, is not 'Should I build a platform?' but primarily 'How should I compete in a world of platforms?'

Instead of becoming digital fashionistas and clutching at everything that seems shiny and modern, we should go back to the core question behind any successful business: 'How can I create meaningful value for my customers and partners?'

With this mindset, some corporate leaders are starting to explore more differentiated ways to create business models for the future without harming the core businesses that deliver value and generate profits today. One aspect of this is looking at the great opportunities for corporates to participate in platforms without building their own.

Health warning: the platform economy is a shapeshifter. Regulators are stepping in with data protection and antitrust laws, for example, and emerging technologies – from APIs to changing operating systems – will redefine what platforms really are. If you play the platform game, watch out for a constantly changing rulebook. Do it well, though, and you will discover plenty of opportunities to be a first mover and even find your own sweet spot to build a proprietary platform.

There are already impressive examples – like China's Ping An, once just a successful insurer, now the centre of an extraordinary web of interconnected businesses – where a whole flock of new, profitable and fast-growing platform-based companies have been created, through corporate venture building, that work in synergy with the parent company. In the last eight years, Ping An has launched five new publicly-listed businesses, with another 15 currently in development. The biggest of these start-ups – a peer-to-peer lending and wealth management company, a health insurance provider and an AI-powered telemedicine service – are currently valued, together, at more than $60 billion. All these new ventures are online service businesses that effectively support and reinforce the core business, generating important new revenue streams, bringing in tens of millions of new customers and allowing Ping An to capture a matchless flow of continuously updated information. Data is the new oil, as the WEF's Martina Larkin says in our foreword, and Ping An knows how to use it, better than almost any other company on Earth.

Ping An ecosystem

So let's take a closer look at the detailed mechanics of platform businesses.

THE RIGHT THING, IN THE RIGHT PLACE, AT THE RIGHT TIME

The most dramatic demonstration of the impact of digitization is the new global dominance of a small handful of platform-based businesses. The beauty of the platform business model is its simplicity – at least in theory. You create new value by bringing together buyers and sellers, customers and products or services, or information and those who need to access it, or by enabling new social relationships. But you don't need to own, or even necessarily control, the products and assets involved.

The most obvious and familiar examples of this are the consumer-facing retail and service companies that have become household names in the last few years. Amazon started life in 1995 as a straightforward online retailer (slogan: 'Earth's biggest bookstore') and is now 'The Everything Store', precisely because it created a platform that enabled anyone to sell through it – as well as Amazon itself. Uber owns no vehicles. Airbnb is effectively the biggest accommodation company in the world, but it owns no property. Even back in 2014, when the world's largest hotel chain, Marriott, announced that it had ambitious plans to add 30,000 rooms over a 12-month period, Airbnb CEO Brian Chesky tweeted back: "We will add that in the next two weeks."

Digital platforms are able to match demand and supply quickly, spontaneously and efficiently, in ways that have never been possible before. Even if they offered no other advantages, that would be a major benefit.

When Covid-19 struck and personal protective equipment (PPE) was desperately needed in the first hotspots – China and Iran, then Italy, Spain, France and the UK – the problem was not just a worldwide shortage of gloves, face masks, gowns and visors. Distribution was haphazard and the PPE that did exist was not in the right places. Chaos ruled for several weeks. PPE was being shipped abroad from factories in the English Midlands while hospitals less than two hours away waited several days for supplies that were due to be flown in from Turkey.

A platform-based ecosystem that's working well provides buyers with a choice of products and suppliers, delivery options and access to competitive prices, while introducing sellers to customers they might otherwise never have reached and generating valuable market data (and usually transaction fees) for the platform owner.

In a global pandemic, if the right data was available, a platform could save lives by bringing scarce medical supplies and healthcare professionals to where they were needed the most. Greek European Parliament member Eva Kaili believes that governments have to work together to gather, monitor and map data relevant to this and other outbreaks: "We need standards for our data measurement, its collection and its sharing." With good information on tap, new platforms could indeed be powerful orchestrators of disaster response. Take a look at the Pfizer case at the end of this section to see what data availability means from a corporate perspective.

If you can piece together a network where every member genuinely derives benefits, large or small, from the connections made through your platform, this ecosystem of independent but interdependent entities will be inherently valuable. If the costs of joining are nil, at least on the consumer side – as with

Facebook, Instagram, TripAdvisor, the Apple App Store and the other examples mentioned above – there will be little to stop new members signing up and the network will expand rapidly.

In the old industrial business model, adding more customers is often a mixed blessing. It invariably adds considerable costs, even in industries where these are just the overheads of providing customer service, maintaining customer records and keeping in contact via mailshots or occasional sales calls.

Enter the seductive idea of 'network effects'. At its core, the theory behind network effects suggests that platforms and products with network effects get better as they get bigger – not just in value to users, but also in accruing more resources to improve their product. The marginal cost of adding a new customer or supplier to an existing network is negligible and the communication needed to keep the relationship alive and up to date comes virtually free. So these businesses are naturally scalable. They can expand quickly, cheaply and without committing new capital or resources. Since the overhead of running the platform can be seen as a fixed cost, the minute share of that cost associated with each individual member of your network actually reduces as the network grows.

This is what leads to the famous Amazon Growth Flywheel, a simple image that is said to have been originally sketched on a restaurant napkin by Jeff Bezos in 1999, when Amazon's early growth was stalling and its original linear business model needed rethinking. Amazon used to buy things, initially books, and then sell them at a profit, like traders have done since the Bronze Age. That meant a big investment in inventory, storage and carrying costs and the constant risk that what Amazon's buyers had bought in would not be what the retail customer would choose to purchase.

The eureka moment for Bezos came when he realized that what customers wanted, above all, was choice. And they didn't care a jot who provided that choice.

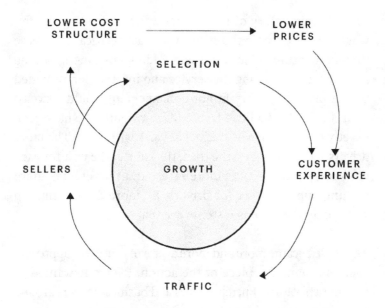

Amazon's growth flywheel

So he took the bold decision to open up the Amazon platform as a marketplace for other sellers – even merchants who would normally be seen as Amazon's direct competitors – with the simple objective of pleasing his buyers and earning their loyalty by giving them the widest possible choice.

If he could offer an almost unlimited selection of products, that would enhance the customer experience and draw in more buyers, which would attract more third-party sellers, which would increase traffic to the site, which would allow Amazon to lower its charges, which would attract more sellers, who would attract more buyers, and so on. The virtuous circle would develop a momentum of its own, and Amazon could grow and grow, virtually without limits.

The crowning glory of this model was that feeding the fly-wheel, at any point in the cycle, would automatically increase this momentum. Whether it was adding customers, adding suppliers or improving the service and information provided by the platform, every minor enhancement would serve to turn the flywheel a little faster. More recently, we have seen exactly the same flywheel effect at work with Uber. The more drivers there are out on the road, the shorter the wait for each customer. That attracts more fares, and that creates more earning opportunities for drivers. So more drivers sign up and the flywheel spins faster every year.

As people became more and more aware of Amazon's approach, everyone wanted a piece of the action. Everyone wanted to become a platform. Entrepreneurs and business leaders around the world crowded into bars, restaurants, or wherever they could find napkins, to scribble their own version of a flywheel, hoping they had just seized their very own Bezos moment. Many are still waiting.

It turns out, surprisingly, that even the platform world isn't flat, but complicated. In fact, there are a wealth of different network effects that depend on the specific needs of the constituents on the two (or more) sides of your platform. There can even be diseconomies of scale. Think of an exclusive dating app – if it aspires to grow further it may have to widen the admission criteria for new members, letting in people who would previously have been excluded and diluting the value proposition for existing users.

What's happening now is that platform players are expanding their activities vertically and horizontally. Amazon and Alibaba started as platforms (orchestrators) but realized that true competitive advantage came when they expanded along the value chain – building up logistics capabilities to further increase customer satisfaction.

Additionally, and this is the bigger move, platforms have begun to expand horizontally across the ecosystem and add more and more areas to their portfolios. They understand that most customers are keen to get more and more services from one source – an integrated experience.

"Take mental illnesses and sleep disorders, for example," Markus Homann of Generali Health Solutions, a corporate venture, explains. "You could offer a separate solution for people with insomnia and another for people with depression, but you will notice that many people with depression also have difficulty sleeping. Being able to interrelate the data flows and the communication is a very big opportunity for improving patient care. People really need integrated care and you have to make it simple for them."

At FoundersLane, we have had several years' experience of corporate venturing with companies across many industries – and with public sector organizations – looking at how they can adopt (and adapt) these principles either to position themselves strongly within a platform or to create their own, where this is sensible.

To start with, especially in complex, regulated industries and industrial B2B, they often feel that they can't, that Amazon and the rest are too distant from the business environment they are in for their example to be relevant. But when we drill down together and look at the challenges they face – such as slow growth, structural friction and lack of innovation in their industries – we find many opportunities for digital technologies and digital platform architectures (niche adaptations of the principles behind Amazon's model) to address them and create paths to new growth and value. We are moving into the age of the industrial internet and it's largely the traditional industries – manufacturing, construction, logistics and so on – that will reap the greatest rewards from changing the ways they work.

KEY AIMS

CREATE EXTRA CONSUMER VALUE
HELP PRODUCERS SUCCEED
ENABLE PREVIOUSLY IMPOSSIBLE TASKS
UNLOCK NEW VALUE ACROSS ECOSYSTEMS

Healthcare is another crucial sector that might certainly gain from thinking in terms of ecosystems and platform-based networks. And the global response to climate change, which, by its nature, has to be cross-sectoral and involve inputs from many different sources and disciplines, could surely benefit from better coordination and higher levels of collaboration than we've seen. Hospitals and doctors, health authorities and national governments, big pharma and small biotech pioneers, universities and funding bodies, distributors and screening laboratories, NGOs and pharmacists, meteorologists and statisticians, agricultural experts and marine biologists, energy suppliers, engineers and even electric car manufacturers are all likely to have important roles to play.

No one knows yet where the answers are going to come from or what form they will take. Within this vast, amorphous ecosystem, merely being able to make contacts and compare notes with specialists from distant disciplines may be the key to sparking innovation and nurturing the thousands of different ideas that are likely to be needed before we hit on the big ones that could shape our destiny and save our planet.

HEROES AND VILLAINS

The world of platform businesses is rapidly changing as technologies (such as the availability of open APIs) and markets are maturing. As we mentioned earlier, the mathematics of network effects have become far more complex since their first described case: the phone system. After the invention of the telephone in 1876, it quickly became obvious that the value of owning a telephone increased dramatically as the number of people on the network grew. People bought phones for their own convenience, but in doing so they added to the usefulness of the telephone for everyone else who had one.

Beyond a certain critical mass, the value customers derived from the service became vastly higher than the cost of joining, a concept that has been formalized in Metcalfe's Law, which states that the value of a telecoms system, as it expands, is eventually proportional to the square of the number of connected users.

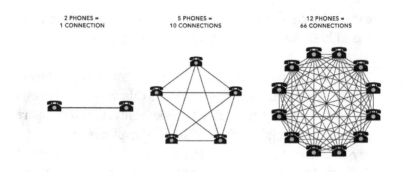

Network effects

In our digital age, we've seen the same kind of network effects at work, first with the World Wide Web itself, then with social networks like Facebook and Twitter, which gain their attraction and influence from the sheer numbers of people connected to and by them. In those cases where the flywheel effect truly applies, adding more customers makes the marketplace more attractive to suppliers; adding more suppliers increases the range of choices on offer and makes it more attractive to customers. Here you have the kind of positive feedback loop that allows spectacularly accelerated growth.

The platform owners monetized this popularity by charging fixed usage fees, or variable commission on transactions, or by selling advertising space to sellers or third parties. In doing so, they began to grow so fast and became so much more profitable than traditional, linear businesses that the top platform-based companies have become the darlings of the investment community, pulling far ahead of the Nasdaq, Dow, FTSE and DAX averages in the last four years.

We don't mean to belittle platforms. On the contrary. With network effects powering their expansion, year after year, these businesses have been able to leverage new technologies, respond to economic and social trends and exploit the hidden value of the abundant and detailed data they generate. They have become immensely powerful, as well as profitable.

But platforms' success – and the near-monopoly positions they hold in many key industries – may not last for ever. As *The Economist* pointed out recently, Apple is now as big as Standard Oil was in the early 1900s (as measured by comparing its global profits with America's GDP), when its ruthlessly anti-competitive actions led the US Supreme Court to order that it should be broken up into three dozen separate and competing oil companies. Anger over the tech giants' sidestepping of tax laws and cavalier attitudes to privacy and political meddling, Facebook's misuse of personal data, and the big players' habit of hoovering up small but potentially troublesome competitors has led many countries to consider using legislation to curb their activities. The EU, which has led the way with its General Data Protection Regulation, is proposing new laws to limit the use of AI and new digital copyright rules. Nearly 30 countries are looking at ideas for digital taxes.

The backlash is on its way. But it's a backlash against the tech leaders' wilful bad behaviour, not their chosen business model. They have already proved the point, beyond doubt, that digital platforms can support extraordinarily fast growth, foster innovative cross-fertilization and tactical agility, and leave more leaden-footed rivals floundering in their wake. Network effects will certainly not cease to fuel the most impressive businesses of the next years. The rules are being rewritten, but there will still be great opportunities for those who develop a deep understanding of a re-emerging game.

YOU CAN'T NOT COMPETE

The problem for long-established businesses, of course, is that they can't just throw the cards up in the air, walk away from their traditional sources of revenue and profit and bet the farm on their ability to pull it off and create an equally profitable and durable digital platform business from scratch. It's not easy to make the kind of radical change that will integrate the platform model into your strategy. Most corporates do not have a properly considered strategy and positioning in respect to building, integrating or partnering with digital platforms.

Incumbent businesses that are inherently static – or, at best, moving forward in linear, incremental steps – are going to be outmanoeuvred, out-thought, outfunded, outpaced and, ultimately, shut out by aggressive, nimble, fast-growing platform-based competitors. Governments and public sector agencies that close their eyes to the challenge of rethinking their roles, responsibilities and delivery mechanisms to take advantage of digital technologies and platform models will find they are even more vulnerable to the savage cost pressures of the post-Covid world than they should be.

Some people believe almost every organization will soon need to be able to demonstrate a platform strategy. Shareholders will demand, they say, that every company they back must have an integrated digital strategy to leverage its strengths and its relationships in a digitized world. Citizens, stung by the higher taxes that are inevitable in the aftermath of the pandemic, will demand that their money is spent in ways that maximize its impact and make their lives better. Business models are not just for business. Platforms are not just for profits.

Whether you should decide to compete *on* platforms or *in* platforms is a separate discussion. The fact is that you cannot compete outside of platforms any longer. The key, as Daimler's Sascha Pallenberg points out, in the case study at the end of this section, is that you must choose your battles carefully.

"This is not about trying to compete with companies that are working on completely different products which are not your core business," he says. "The route to success is focusing on what you are good at, evolving all the time and getting the right partners."

In fact, playing on a platform can be very profitable indeed. Apple's App Store has created opportunities for app developers worldwide and spawned a wealth of jobs.

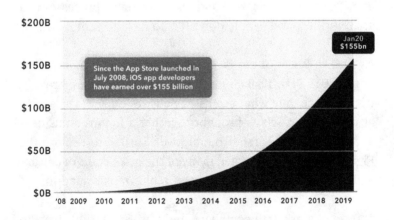

Since the App Store launched in July 2008, iOS app developers have earned over $155 billion

Jan20
$155bn

Apple's app store is a goldmine for developers

ADAPTED FROM STATISTA

95

Even if you get the strategic thinking right, creating a transformational business model based on platforms and ecosystem orchestration is always going to need wholehearted commitment, careful planning and fast, sure-footed execution. Changing any long-established organization – especially a successful one – is difficult. Just making that commitment to look at radically new alternatives is hard enough as a first step. However, with the rise of hybrid platforms, which combine parts that are either asset-heavy or asset-light (such as IoT and digital), hardware-oriented players can find new entry points into existing ecosystems. The healthcare industry, with its traditional reliance on physical assets and labour, is one example of a sector where hybrid platforms will be particularly common.

Over time, organizations develop their own powerful immune systems, with a strong defensive bias in favour of the status quo. They have their tried and tested systems, processes and assumptions, and people don't like to have to rethink them.

As Annika Brack of the World Economic Forum pointed out at the 2019 FightBack Summit in Berlin, people are brought up not to change what seems to be working. Conversations at the summit, which brought together a hundred business and technology leaders from all over Europe to explore the FightBack agenda, revealed many of the fine details of culture and attitude that get in the way of rapid transformation.

"I used to work with engineers, and it was incredibly hard to explain the necessity to change," said Brack. "There is a 'Never touch a running system' mentality that is hard to overcome."

Most managers' habits of thought are built on past experience, based on what they have seen work throughout their careers.

But radical change can only happen when an organization's leaders steel themselves to peer into the future and accept that tomorrow's world will be a very different place.

In the extraordinary circumstances that nudged the Earth out of its orbit in early 2020, people split two ways. Some became immersed in a nostalgic yearning for the apparent certainties of the world that had gone, the lost world of 2019. Others reeled at the shock of what was happening, dusted themselves down and started thinking, bravely and imaginatively, about the changed society that might be built out of the grief and the economic wreckage. Whole industries had been stopped in their tracks for months on end. Jobs had been lost, as well as countless lives. Was there any chance that we could shape things better as we worked our way back to find the new normal?

There should be. But nothing will ever be quite the same. This is a new environment we are living in now. It will create entirely new threats and opportunities and it will need a new approach to innovation.

Instead of trying to identify the next logical step forward, doing conventional research to minimize the risks and then focusing on executing it efficiently and professionally – the traditional route to new product development – organizations will need to embrace uncertainty. They will need to admit that picking the right idea to pursue is going to be harder than ever. Managers trained to think of line extensions and brand extensions as low-risk ways to find new customers and capture new revenue will need to learn fast that playing safe is a dangerous game.

Instead of one new change factor, the digital revolution, we now have two. In the new, post-Covid digital world, the rules have changed again. You need to have a clear view of how the business you're in will change in the next five or ten years, and to re-conceive both your role within it and your place in society as a whole.

You need to think big. One favourite Silicon Valley question is, 'How high is up?' In other words, if a particular idea really did catch fire and reach its full potential, just how big could that potential be? An equally valid, but less publicly hyped, question would be 'How broad is wide?' While some players are trying to capture everything within one vertical, others are trying to move around horizontally to cover the needs of their customers. Welcome to ecosystem thinking, the topic of our next section.

WHAT'S YOUR ROLE IN THE ECOSYSTEM?

One crucial unfair advantage that could work in your favour is your established place in your sector's ecosystem, that shifting web of companies that compete, collaborate and combine in many different ways to deliver the practical bundles of products and services that consumers and businesses want.

Virtually unheard of as a business concept a few years ago, ecosystems have become especially prominent since Apple threw its App Store open to external developers in 2008. At that time, it offered 500 apps. By early 2020, there were more than 2 million, and Apple had paid out a total of $155 billion to developers.

Apple knows exactly where it is positioned in its ecosystem – slap bang in the middle. But it may not be quite as obvious exactly where you fit into your business environment. And it is always a useful exercise to work out where you sit, whether it's right at the heart of a digital ecosystem or in some specialized and secure niche (which is often, incidentally, an admirably secure and defensible place to be). Your existing assets, including your technologies, talents, connections, brand and data, provide a good starting point for thinking about finding your unique place in the ecosystem. Just be aware that some assets might be surprisingly valuable in the digital space, even if you've never thought of them as being significant.

The big ecosystem players know where they are, of course. As they grow, they tend to expand not only vertically along the product or service value chain, but also horizontally around the customer. One prime example is Chinese insurance provider Ping An, which has successfully deployed advanced technologies to move outwards from financial services into sectors ranging from healthcare and auto sales to real estate and smart city services.

The following diagram illustrates how companies can think about positioning themselves vertically and horizontally in the various dimensions of importance to an individual customer and create a seamless experience powered by shared data. Health experts among our readers will notice that the dimensions include the major categories of social determinants of health. Indeed, if companies aim to positively affect these aspects of people's lives, the chances are that they will genuinely enhance their health and their quality of life.

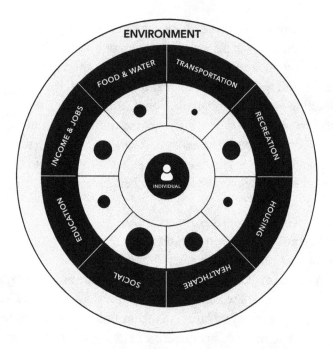

Positioning based on the individual's needs

MORE INFORMATION ON WWW.JOINFIGHTBACK.COM

Apple's experience with the App Store ecosystem is not unique. Ecosystems are making their presence felt in many industries, and they could be destined to radically reshape our business world, with devastating speed. Already the borders between industries are beginning to blur or disappear and that process can only be accelerated by the disruption and realignments triggered by the Covid pandemic. In late 2017, McKinsey forecast that today's 100-plus industries and value chains would collapse into just 12 gigantic ecosystems, accounting for one-third of the world's business revenue, by 2025.

McKinsey was probably overstating both the speed and extent of the change. But this prediction was surely on the right lines when it talked of a dramatic shakedown leading to a relatively small number of very big industry groupings – "a few large orchestrators, big winners, and a huge shift of wealth and value creation".

'HOPING FOR A, WHILE REWARDING B'

There is a dark side, of course, to the future McKinsey envisages, with just a dozen monster ecosystems dominating global business activity. Any concentration of power in the hands of a small number of profit-driven entities is potentially dangerous for society and against the interests of the world's nations and their citizens. That's why civilized countries have competition regulations and antitrust laws and, increasingly, regulatory requirements to guarantee that switching and interoperability are not obstructed by dominant suppliers.

So far, the visible effects of ecosystem thinking have been largely benign. We are seeing many examples of genuinely collaborative, more or less self-regulating ecosystems – such as those around the Android and iOS operating systems and their vast shoals of useful apps – that seem to benefit all the participants and the customers as well.

But it could all go wrong. In the new digitally-enabled ecosystems, some orchestrators, because they have unique access to the data, may well try to make sure they are the customer's first touchpoint. This would bestow upon them the power to decide what customers got, and when and how they got it, giving them disproportionate influence within the ecosystem. This could lead to a drastic shift of value across the value chain and the rapid emergence of monopolistic winner-takes-all outcomes.

It is clear that one of the problems in all this is the big question of incentives and externalities.

If companies are allowed to act as if profit was the only good, they will be incentivized to maximize profits with no regard for any harmful side-effects of their activities. If the external consequences of an action – the carbon emissions from the fuel that's burned when you fly off for your holiday to Venice, for example – are not reflected in the price paid for your ticket, the airline is getting a free ride at the expense, ultimately, of the citizen and the environment. Mining operations that pollute rivers, clothing sweatshops in developing countries that don't look after their workers and companies that litter the oceans with single-use packaging – they are all able to make profits because they don't have to pay the full costs that are being incurred.

Some of the finest business thinkers of our age, including Professor Rita McGrath of Columbia Business School, bestselling author of *Seeing Around Corners* and *The End of Competitive Advantage*, have focused on this dangerous temptation as a major flaw in the way we currently do business.

When we talked to McGrath for this book, she was emphatic about the need to look again at the balance between incentives and outcomes.

"We have to think about what the incentives are," she said. "There's a wonderful article by Steven Kerr called 'On the Folly of Hoping for A, While Rewarding B'. We're doing an awful lot of that right now."

In the US, she pointed out, the Covid crisis has underlined the clash between the administration's desire to keep its people and economy safe and its belief, "unique in the developed world", that government has no business being involved in healthcare.

"That's weird. A lot of other countries have a more systems-based approach, because you have a provider who can actually have a window into the whole system. In the US, it's a much harder challenge, because it's so fragmented."

Energetic, purposeful innovation is going to be one of the important factors in the recovery from the pandemic. But there is an aftermath of shock and confusion, and a lot of apparent certainties have been called into question.

"This virus has thrown everyone's assumptions into disarray," she said. "In this environment, all the leaders of nations and businesses have been shoved into a situation of high uncertainty.

"But I'm used to that. I study innovation and entrepreneurship, so I've spent my working life dealing with high uncertainty. That's my world."

The problem is partly that today's leaders don't recognize how different entrepreneurial innovation is from the more familiar disciplines of running the sort of solid, established organization that keeps production lines going or makes trains run safely and on time.

"They don't understand that the innovation process is a numbers game," Rita McGrath told us. "You've got to think about the *rate* of failure versus the *cost* of failure.

"People who optimize an existing business are primed to minimize the *rate* of failure. What entrepreneurs optimize for is the *cost* of failure. You need to start 50, 100, maybe 200 things to get something that's really robust. They don't understand that if you can keep the cost of failing low and you can do it really quickly, you can have a gazillion failures and it doesn't matter."

One of the strengths of platform-based ecosystems is their ability to take on board and exploit the fruits of participants' innovation. Unlike traditional manufacturers or wholesalers, ecosystem orchestrators don't have to predict demand, and they don't even have to pretend that they can supply – or even guess at – the entire range of products and services customers may desire. They simply make a multitude of channels available for supply and demand to seek each other out, allowing third-party providers to link up with buyers seamlessly, across the platform, to deliver whatever businesses or consumers turn out to want.

The orchestrators don't own the ecosystem – nobody does. But they own the connection, and that connection is the key. The traditional Marxist emphasis on the ownership of the means of production is not as important now as it used to be. It's control of the means of distribution that has become the dominant factor.

Different industries have different ecosystems, and many of them are changing fast, especially post-Covid. Personal transport – the business of getting from A to B – had already seen a lot of changes in the last few years. Social trends, such as the increasing popularity of cycling, the growth of car-sharing services like Zipcar and the impact of Uber, Lyft and Grab, were already shifting the dynamics and reducing car ownership. Many of the lockdown cyclists will no doubt revert to four wheels over the next few months, but our relationship with our cars will probably never be quite the same again, and few commuters will be as happy as they used to be about cramming onto packed trains and buses. For the organizations, public and private, involved in the personal mobility ecosystem, these shifts in attitude will create new opportunities and challenges, opening up new possibilities for innovative products and services.

In the same way, we may see patients becoming a lot less keen to waste their time and risk infection sitting in crowded waiting rooms at doctors' surgeries or emergency clinics at hospitals. Telephone triage and video consultations are bound to become more popular, and there may be many other changes in the who, when and where of primary healthcare delivery and in other parts of the medical ecosystem.

Venture capitalist Marc Andreessen, the inventor of Netscape Navigator, the first practical internet browser, and founder of Andreessen Horowitz, sees this kind of unannounced tectonic shift as the spark for many high-value innovations. He believes it is important to watch out for trends like this and be ready to follow them up. "The big secular trends do drive a lot of what happens in the VC industry – things like mobile and cloud and social," he says. "But the big things don't always look that big at the beginning. It's only afterwards they look obvious."

Because of the damping effects of regulation, the narrative healthcare entrepreneurs have to tell their investors these days doesn't sound quite as promising as those in other industries, like social media and e-commerce. But healthcare has seen the rise of some impressive $1 billion-plus 'unicorns' recently. And while it is not all about creating unicorns, there are many formidable problems to solve where the right solution could still generate profits and make the world a better place.

If we keep mentioning healthcare and climate, it's because these markets are particularly well suited to the corporate venture building approach, which enables new digital businesses to piggyback on the parent organization's assets to overcome high barriers to entry and scaling problems (as discussed in Section 1).

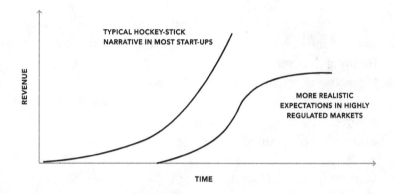

Healthcare entrepreneurs can't pitch the same hyperscaling stories as entrepreneurs in social media and e-commerce

A NEW WAY FORWARD

Most organizations aren't built for change. They may spend a lot of time talking about it, but they don't know how to make the first move.

In many large organizations, including multinational corporations, future leaders can rise up through the finance or operations functions and arrive in the boardroom never having had any contact at all with entrepreneurship or innovation. Many are grossly ill-equipped to develop new strategies that challenge the status quo or change the company's direction. So when society changes and markets shift, they gradually get left behind.

It happened to General Electric. It happened to IBM and Kodak and Alcoa. It was even happening at Microsoft, until a visionary former R&D man, Satya Nadella, was appointed as CEO in 2014.

And when there is an abrupt and wholly unforeseen disaster, like the coronavirus scourge, very few leaders have the background and determination to meet it head-on and think creatively about what is to follow.

Transforming your business model begins with a willingness to recognize that turning strategy into action is always uncomfortable. It means reallocating your finite resources – capital, people and time and attention – which means that some areas of today's business will necessarily get less of them. One reason so few companies ever achieve dramatic growth is that the vast majority allocate their budgets the same way, in roughly the same proportions, every single year. The temptation for mature businesses is always to invest in the same things: productivity improvements, digitizing existing processes, a bit of geographical expansion, some new products and services, perhaps some M&A activity. Innovation – creating the future – tends to get a small share of what's left over.

This is something the experts in this area have been grappling with for years. Our experience of working with corporations and public sector bodies has led us to understand many of these inhibitions and constraints that make it hard for top executives to get to grips with the need for innovation. But it has also helped us develop a practical and proportionate approach to corporate venture building that enables large organizations to break out of the rut, inject entrepreneurial and innovative flair into their operations and build a portfolio of digital product and service ideas from which new and scalable businesses can grow.

We will explore the advantages of this new methodology – and a key component of it we call 'hybrid entrepreneurship'– later in the book, in Section 5. For now, what's important to know is that it is a new form of partnership between experienced technology entrepreneurs and large organizations that carefully protects and actively exploits the unique strengths of both sides.

This best-of-both-worlds corporate venture building approach allows traditional corporations to build and scale innovative new businesses, often based on platform business models, that capitalize on what the parent company does best but also have the tools and capabilities to survive and thrive on their own.

The established organization's contribution will include a range of physical and intellectual assets no start-up could enjoy, including capital, domain expertise, market knowledge, workforce skills, brand reputation, historical data, software, trademarks and patents.

Less obviously, the new venture will also be able to leverage the organization's relational capital – its relationships with current and prospective customers, partners, investors, suppliers, developers and even governments. This network of formal and informal relationships is often an essential element in ensuring the fast growth of a new business, especially in complex, regulated sectors like healthcare. In this context, the digital platform can be seen as a new piece of business technology that specifically helps you exploit relational capital.

Corporate venture building is very different from the standard corporate venture capital model, in which the established company is more or less a passive investor. It involves a much greater commitment and a more active role for all participants, with the potential for far more strategically significant outcomes, and it could be a key ingredient in mastering the new normal.

We have identified a great need and a great opportunity in this area. Adopting a structured, disciplined and effective methodology that combines the strengths of large organizations with the creativity, tech expertise and drive of experienced and motivated entrepreneurs can make it possible to launch digital businesses that will grow fast, earn profits and serve the parent company's long-term strategic aims.

> "We need to inspire a new generation of leaders that can be nuanced enough to understand that when you build a product, you've got to create a product that is algorithmically efficient but also takes into consideration the human impact. You have to be bilingual in that regard – technologically lingual and humanly lingual!"
>
> GERARD GRECH
> CEO OF TECH NATION, A GROWTH PLATFORM
> FOR TECH COMPANIES AND LEADERS

Every project has different objectives, ambitions and metrics, but this approach has been proving its worth for several years now and its effectiveness is beyond question. We have seen hybrid leadership – managing the core organization and creating the new normal – delivering results that transform whole organizations and continuing to generate game-changing ideas that will create and capture value for years to come.

As you will recognize, we are at a crucial inflection point, where society's biggest challenges in relation to climate and health are met with new technological possibilities. Through carefully chosen examples, you will also gain an understanding, if you don't have one already, of just why the opportunities emerging from these circumstances are so difficult to seize.

If only there was something that would instil the right sense of urgency ...

KEY CONCEPTS

1. THE FLYWHEEL DEFECT
Network effects have long been hailed as offering the Holy Grail of business strategies. They can certainly be powerful, but the devil, as always, is in the detail.

2. A PLATFORM OF PLATFORMS?
While many companies still grapple with the basic arithmetic around platforms, others are already expanding horizontally, guided by user needs. Some of these ecosystem players have started to build meta-platforms.

3. THE OTHER GAME CHANGERS
As platform markets mature, the rules are being rewritten, again. Only this time it's being done – at least partly – by the regulators.

OUR KEY RECOMMENDATIONS FOR YOU:

- You may do best to stick to your core competencies and excel at playing on a platform, rather than trying to be a platform. Daimler has shown how well this can work. For some, becoming a platform will be the right strategy. Others may join forces with other players within an ecosystem. The big questions are how to stay relevant and how to do it – partnering, buying or building?

- Don't assume that creating a platform is always the right answer. "If you build it, they will come" is usually no more than a Hollywood dream. The dynamics of complex situations and B2B trading can be quite unlike those that powered Amazon's rise to the top.

- Keep an eye open for the growing influence of 'hybrid platforms' that manage to combine asset-light and asset-heavy elements.

- Platform businesses shouldn't only be disintermediators, optimizing supply and demand in a single sector. There's a growing need for horizontal integration, offering one-stop-shop services for all of a customer's needs. Your ability to exploit synergies between separate services within an ecosystem may be your competitive advantage.

- The rules around platform markets are in a state of flux. Watch what's going on and do what you can to influence the way regulators view platforms. Within the ever-changing rules of the game, there may well be scope for you to jump in, just as there is for your competitors.

PFIZER BENEFITS FROM 'WIN-WIN' CO-CREATION PROGRAMME

Pfizer is a huge multinational pharma company, innovative, acquisitive and highly successful, with 2018 revenues of $53.6 billion. Its products – including popular cholesterol-reducing statins and erectile dysfunction treatments – are among the world's best-known and most widely-used drugs.

Yet even Pfizer is changing the way it operates in response to the pressures and opportunities of digitization, as Peter Albiez explained to us. Albiez joined Pfizer 24 years ago, as a pharmaceuticals consultant, and rose through the ranks via senior positions in sales and marketing. For the last three years, he has played a major role in shaping the company's destiny as the Country Manager for Pfizer Germany.

The pharmaceutical industry is absolutely dependent on innovation. Traditionally, new medicines have been developed in two main ways. They either emerge from the work done in the big pharma companies' research laboratories around the world, or they are created by small, specialized firms, often venture capital-backed start-ups, which will eventually be acquired or sell the rights to their discoveries to a larger company before the expensive (and often disappointing) phase of repeated clinical trials.

Despite advances in technology and our understanding of biological systems, the chances of any new compound proving itself to be safe and effective through several stages of clinical trials and coming to market are extremely small. Even today's computer-aided drug design techniques can't remove the need to explore a broad portfolio of options in the hope of finding a single viable product.

Five years ago, Pfizer began a new programme specifically aimed at collaborating and co-creating with start-ups. The idea was to combine the big company's experience, know-how or facilities – offering a customized approach to the needs of start-ups – with the very different assets the digital entrepreneurs could bring to the table.

These assets – Albiez cites fresh thinking, tech skills, agility and speed – have injected a new dynamism into the drug research process. And the results have been remarkable. Despite the potential culture clashes involved, Pfizer has benefited enormously from this initiative.

"After five years of experience in collaborating with start-ups, we can absolutely state that, if set up the right way, this is a win-win endeavour," says Albiez.

One vital element in this is the enormous amount of data the senior partner can bring to bear on their joint efforts. No small company, acting alone, would be able to access such a wealth of detail about patients, compounds and treatment methods. Within the collaborative framework Pfizer has established, this information has been a key asset, providing clues to new approaches and helping the researchers avoid wasting time pursuing false trails.

"I'm convinced that data is a tremendous treasure that can help us in accelerating the development of diagnostics and new medicines and providing better prevention and care," says Albiez.

Pfizer believes digitization will fundamentally change the nature of healthcare, empowering patients to take more control of their wellbeing and medical conditions, and helping the pharmaceutical industry research, develop and manufacture innovative drugs and services to improve patient outcomes.

For Albiez, that means grasping "a multitude of opportunities to support and enhance our purpose". The successful start-up collaboration programme is just one element in a radical reshaping of the way the company works.

"Digitization needs to serve the people, not vice versa," he says. "Digitization means tremendous change, which might also lead to uncertainty, and we all have an obligation to proactively manage this transformation.

"It is a strategic priority for Pfizer to be part of the digital transformation, to drive new opportunities and to think digital in every step of our value generation for patients."

RESHAPING THE BUSINESS MODEL FOR THE DIGITAL AGE

Karthik Suri's career is all about fanning sparks into wildfires, getting big results fast. He achieves this by helping companies build scale, drive growth and manage the growth profitably (often a major challenge) through strategic clarity, strong operational results and an insistence on an inclusive culture. In a whirlwind three years as the COO of GE Digital, from 2017 to 2020, he was responsible for driving strategic growth planning, business operations and a string of imaginative transformational initiatives.

Karthik Suri and Felix Staeritz have known each other for a long time. They are both members of the World Economic Forum's Digital Platforms and Ecosystems Executive Working Group. When he arrived at GE Digital, after a decade with platform companies like eBay, Yahoo! and PayPal, Suri found himself at a traditional industrial giant that had been struggling to address the need for large-scale digital transformation for several years.

In 2008 – more than 120 years after its founding – GE was still one of the world's industrial leaders. As productivity gains across most sectors began to slow down, GE's executives had seen the opportunity to gain efficiency by unlocking the industrial data being generated by its machines and systems. GE pioneered a new way of thinking about industrial computing that used asset and system data to drive transformative changes across a range of different vertical markets.

Much of its early work helped define the Industrial
Internet of Things (IIoT) space, and GE assumed a
leadership position as a platform-based software and
data analytics company.

With sensors integrated into all kinds of machines
providing continuous streams of information, Big
Data analysis could be used to optimize productivity,
improve health and reliability and introduce cost-
saving predictive maintenance programmes. Cautious
pundits said the market for an industrial internet platform and applications could be worth $225 billion by
2020. Others said it could be worth as much as $500
billion. So the prize was enormous, and GE invested in
building and launching Predix, its cloud-based plat-
form-as-a-service, as well as industrial applications like
its Asset Performance Management and Operations
Performance Management suites.

"We started off with a software centre of excellence,
aimed at building digital capabilities that would bring
productivity benefits for our GE businesses," says Suri.

"As we saw early success in this space, we started
to make these capabilities available through the GE
businesses in the industrial verticals where they had
long-established history and domain expertise.
In parallel, we started selling into other industries
like consumer goods, automotive and food and bever-
age production.

"We started on this journey to improve our own
operations, and we wound up productizing that knowledge and offering it to businesses well beyond our

own footprint. Essentially, we moved from projects to products to a portfolio of products with a foundational digital platform."

The journey has been tough, though, and as with any trip into unknown territory, there have been lessons to be learned. GE had set out to build its own data centres and its own cloud infrastructure, before finally realizing that it made more sense to run Predix on public cloud services, while focusing its efforts on data and content, like applications and analytics that are specific to particular industrial segments.

Realizing early on that large-scale digital transformation of the industry was too large an undertaking for one company, GE was keen to build out the ecosystem and get large numbers of developers and other third-party contributors using the Predix platform.

But it soon learned that industrial customers were more interested in a highly focused ecosystem that offered trusted partners, actionable insights and faster outcomes for their specific problems – not a vast app store to explore. The initial focus on the total number of developers was, Suri says, "a vanity metric".

Even if it sometimes stumbled on the path, GE Digital has continued leading the way. While some of the GE business units are doing very well, the company is still under considerable pressure – chairman and CEO Lawrence Culp recently called 2019 "a reset year for us" – though GE's digital businesses are growing and driving real results for their customers.

"One good thing there was that everyone shared an understanding that there are enormous risks in clinging to the status quo," says Suri.

"They see there's tremendous untapped potential in this Internet of Things-delivered, platform-enabled technology. People there have that common purpose, the shared vision of how unlocking data can provide actionable insights and optimize assets and operations."

Transformational change is hard, and it needs the right business model and structures to make it happen. GE Digital has progressed from a software centre of excellence to a business unit with its own P&L, tightly aligned with the other GE businesses.

"This is a massive shift in the business model," says Suri. "You have a different mindset if you are a global technology product and platform company that's keen on driving its own growth and its customers' growth.

"You are abstracting common themes in products and building capabilities that are interoperable and extendable and that transcend the immediate use case. We had to get there through a process of evolution and learning along the way, and GE is well positioned now as more and more customers are taking those crucial first steps towards the IIoT."

THE BURGER THEORY OF INNOVATION MANAGEMENT

Sascha Pallenberg lives and breathes mobility. Besides being one of the most influential bloggers and journalists in the area of mobile computing worldwide, he's walking the talk, constantly travelling between Asia, the US and Europe. At least, in the pre-Covid days. He's been named one of the European digital industry's 100 Top Influencers and one of the top 100 most important Germans online. Joining Daimler as Head of Digital Transformation in 2017, he fuelled his passion for the intersection of mobility and the digital world. Since the coronavirus pandemic struck, he has been busy thinking about what entrepreneurial strategies businesses can employ to compete in a post-Covid world.

Business has fundamentally changed in the last few months. Corporations are looking at the ways they conducted business before and how those practices can be improved upon as we move forward, and Pallenberg is passionate about disproving those detractors who say that German carmakers have been slow to adapt.

As a realist, he knows a big corporation simply cannot manoeuvre as quickly as a start-up. But he sees the ideal as being a hybrid organization combining elements of the corporate and start-up cultures.

"It is important not to try to bring a start-up culture into a corporation – not to do something that is just not possible when you have 300,000 colleagues all around the world. That's not going to happen," he says.

But Daimler is far from set in its ways. A decade ago, it saw the need for car-sharing services and got involved in mobility start-ups like mytaxi and moovel. Altogether, it's investing €30 billion in backing e-mobility initiatives. It has also pumped money into AI companies and battery technology start-ups, and it is looking to the future in a big way, with major sustainability commitments. Daimler will have only carbon-neutral production in all its plants by 2022, meaning that all the energy that's used will come from sustainable sources. The whole company aims to be carbon-neutral, from top to bottom, by 2039, eleven years ahead of the zero-carbon targets set in the Paris Climate Agreement.

The history of Daimler's involvement in electric vehicles goes back to 1907, when it made its first electric trucks for the Berlin Fire Department. By 2025, every model in the range will be electrified, whether as a mixed-fuel hybrid, a plug-in hybrid or a fully electric vehicle. Along the way, though, Daimler made one other significant contribution to the evolution of electric driving in 2014 when it put investment money into Elon Musk's Tesla, which was bankrupt at the time.

Along with its investments in electric mobility, the company is working to make the whole value chain – 3,000 to 5,000 different components, depending on the car – carbon neutral. Everything from the raw material from mines in Central Africa, including how it is shipped and transported, will be carbon neutral. Pallenberg admits it will be a huge challenge, but Daimler is already talking to its suppliers about making carbon-neutral production a reality. Sustainability is vital for the planet, he says, but also "a compelling sales argument".

Businesses must think smarter, not harder. But even Daimler's army of 20,000 engineers can't come up with all the technologies and innovations it needs. So it is impossible to compete on your own and imperative to find the right partners. Daimler has teamed up with Microsoft, tapping into the US firm's expertise in optimizing and analysing data to build exceptional voice assistance features for drivers.

"You do need to know where your competencies are," says Pallenberg. "You need to know what your core business is. But that doesn't it's right to stand still."

"This is the time for managers to think outside the box and embrace the entrepreneurial spirit. As we proceed in a reconfigured world where old ideas may not work much longer, it helps to imagine the corporation as a hamburger," says Pallenberg.

At the top, you have the bun, or top management. These people are in contact with market research, heads of development and engineering and business analysts, and they define the strategy for the company. On the bottom bun, there are less experienced colleagues, just entering the corporate environment.

The patty in the middle is senior management, and this layer often faces the biggest challenge in keeping an open mind and embracing new ideas. Senior managers may well be conditioned to do things a certain way and resist change, saying, "We all do it this way. We always did it this way."

Pallenberg has navigated around that problem at Daimler by inviting managers to cross-specialism lunches with a range of colleagues from different departments, like R&D, production and engineering, and having them discuss together why Daimler stopped building its original three-wheeled vehicle from 1886. Just because it was the way they did it, that did not mean they always had to do it that way. "You've got to stimulate and reinvigorate management at all levels," says Pallenberg, "because without the patty you just won't have a hamburger."

Sometimes it takes a hard push to make change happen. Only about 4% of Germans worked from home prior to 2020. Many managers told employees it was simply not possible. But at the peak of the Covid-19 lockdown measures, that number rose to 21%. When it came to it, many companies were able to make it work perfectly well.

Pallenberg, who is based in Taiwan and spends much of the year travelling, admits that the pandemic has brought him some personal benefits.

"For the first time in 15 years, I've been in one place for three consecutive months. That has never, ever happened to me before, and you know what? I love it."

It's given him time to think about some of the big topics, like leadership, change and innovation.

"We need to have a different mindset when it comes to leadership – embracing change, constantly embracing change, preaching the gospel that change is good for you, and that the fundamental idea of each and every technology we're bringing to the markets is to make the world a better place.

"Because that's why engineers and developers start to build something, and it's also why entrepreneurs start to build new businesses. It's because they want to change something."

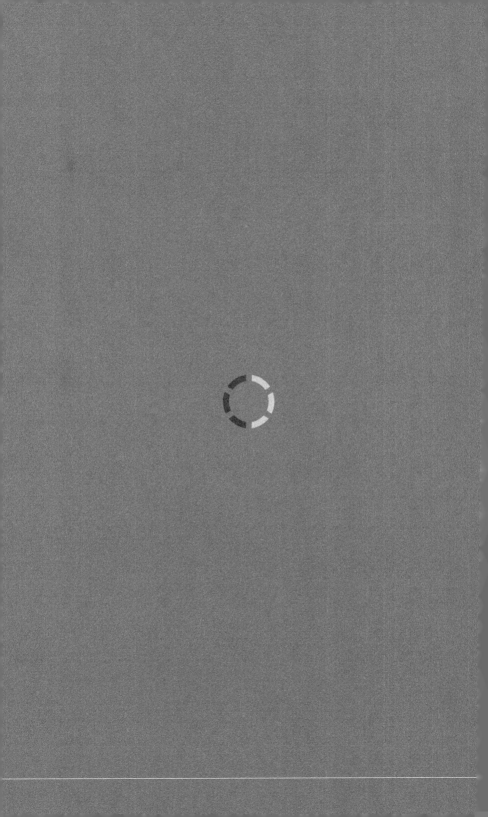

SECTION 3

THIS ISN'T JUST ABOUT BUSINESS
OPPORTUNITIES ANY MORE.
WE NEED TO LEVERAGE OUR
ASSETS TO SURVIVE

WE'D NEED A LOCKDOWN EVERY YEAR

In early 2020, while citizens in countries around the world were confined to their homes and death, fear and economic mayhem stalked the streets, the environment had its first holiday for many years.

With cars parked and airlines grounded, factories and retail outlets closed and almost all normal business and social activity on hold, there was a huge fall in emissions of the carbon dioxide and greenhouse gases responsible for global warming.

Detailed analysis published by *Nature: Climate Change* in late May pointed to an estimated peak reduction in CO_2 emissions (around 7 April) of 17%, compared with 2019 levels.

This was based on an international study of data from 69 countries, led by Professor Corinne Le Quéré, of the UK's University of East Anglia, and involving experts from Stanford University in the US, Norway's Cicero Centre and research units in the Netherlands, France, Germany and Australia.

The net effect of the emission reductions could be up to about 7%, the study said, if government-imposed restrictions were tapered off gradually towards the end of the year. This would take overall emissions back to levels last seen in 2006.

But the shock news embedded in these figures is that this spectacular reduction in activity will need to be repeated every single year for several decades if we are going to limit global warming to 1.5°C.

In other words, just locking down hundreds of millions of people, taking traffic off the roads and virtually halting aviation and large chunks of industry for months – as a one-off – won't have saved our world. We'd need to do it over and over again, or find some other way.

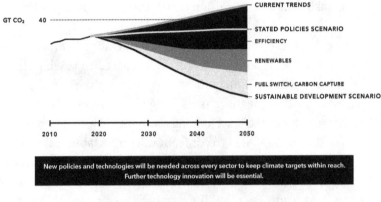

GT CO₂   40 ....

CURRENT TRENDS

STATED POLICIES SCENARIO
EFFICIENCY

RENEWABLES

FUEL SWITCH, CARBON CAPTURE
SUSTAINABLE DEVELOPMENT SCENARIO

2010   2020   2030   2040   2050

New policies and technologies will be needed across every sector to keep climate targets within reach.
Further technology innovation will be essential.

Energy-related CO₂ emission reductions in sustainable development scenario, by source

MORE INFORMATION ON WWW.JOINFIGHTBACK.COM
IEA, 2019

"Behavioural change is not enough," said Le Quéré.

"These extreme decreases are likely to be temporary, as they do not reflect structural changes in the economic, transport or energy systems. But if we take this opportunity to put structural changes in place, we've now seen what it's possible to achieve."

Since annual lockdowns are not going to be making a contribution, it is clear now – if it wasn't before – that the scale of the action needed to save the planet is enormous.

Irrespective of the details of the specific plans and actions that are put in place, it is obvious that our response to climate breakdown must be coordinated, collaborative, ambitious, imaginative and massively well funded. It must be political and technological, made up of vast, daring initiatives and thousands of small, innovative improvements to the way we live and work, provide for our needs and solve our day-to-day problems. If we fail, we all fail. The world is irredeemably interdependent, and it's irredeemably doomed, if we don't make this our highest priority.

That sounds like lofty rhetoric. But what does it mean in practice? It means we will have to be prepared to pay higher taxes. Having more money in our pockets in the short term will mean nothing if there is no long term to enjoy it in. It means we will have to start judging our political leaders on the basis of their willingness to confront uncomfortable realities.

One of the lessons of the coronavirus nightmare has been the unexpected readiness of millions of people of many different nations to accept and adhere to severe restrictions on their personal freedom. That was something we wouldn't necessarily have wanted to bet on. Lockdowns, social distancing, self-isolation and quarantine measures have been largely successful in getting people off the streets. But Covid-19 has been very close, sudden and immediate. The daily death figures have been horrific. People have known people who became ill. Many families have been touched by death. The threat has been all too obvious.

Climate breakdown feels more remote. We know there have been more and bigger storms, and hotter, drier summers. Around the world, eight of the ten hottest years on record have happened in the last decade. But most of us have still not been brought face to face with the grim realities of where we are heading.

Rising sea levels and coastal flooding are urgent issues for people in Bangladesh and the Maldives. They don't loom so large for the citizens of Berlin or Paris, London or LA, Sydney, Beijing or Moscow. Climatic changes that increase transmission of malaria, dengue fever and cholera in Africa and Asia seem like a distant problem.

Climate events like Hurricane Maria, which hit Puerto Rico in 2017, causing devastation and many deaths, are obviously tragic, but they can seem very far away. Puerto Rico is an American territory, but it's way down in the Caribbean, a thousand miles southeast of Florida. Yet Puerto Rico's disaster directly touched the lives of hospital patients and staff across the US mainland, as the destruction of the islands' factories knocked out America's main source of intravenous fluid bags. For months afterwards, with no IV bags available, nurses had to spend many hours standing at the bedside, slowly injecting medications by syringe instead of putting up drips to treat the sick people in their care.

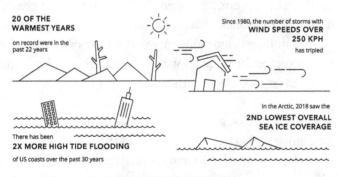

20 OF THE WARMEST YEARS on record were in the past 22 years

Since 1980, the number of storms with **WIND SPEEDS OVER 250 KPH** has tripled

There has been **2X MORE HIGH TIDE FLOODING** of US coasts over the past 30 years

In the Arctic, 2018 saw the **2ND LOWEST OVERALL SEA ICE COVERAGE**

ADAPTED FROM RISKMETHODS.NET

In fact, healthcare itself, as it is currently delivered, is a substantial part of the climate change problem. It is already responsible for 4.6% of global emissions and that figure is rising steadily. The biggest contributors of all are fairly predictable – electricity and heating (30%), transport (15%), manufacturing and construction (14%) and agriculture (11%). But hospitals use a lot of energy, create a lot of waste and generate a lot of potentially unnecessary journeys that could be avoided if we moved to a more decentralized delivery system.

THE DOCTOR WILL HEAR YOU NOW

This is one point where the twin issues of healthcare and climate change clearly coincide. Decentralization of healthcare, at every level, is a desirable development that has been given a sudden and unexpected boost by the impact of the coronavirus pandemic.

People who were ill or had accidents while Covid-19 rampaged across the world were very reluctant to go to hospital or visit their family doctor. Responsible citizens were anxious not to place any unnecessary burdens on struggling health facilities and nobody wanted to risk catching the virus while sitting in a doctor's waiting room. An overloaded system that had creaked and groaned for decades was suddenly forced to improvise new ways of handling minor ailments and injuries and providing advice and care for patients with long-term conditions. And, in many cases, it adapted rather well.

Within a few weeks, general practitioners in many countries were dealing with a large proportion of their day-to-day work via the telephone. Both GPs and hospitals introduced rough and ready video consultations, using Zoom, Skype or WhatsApp, and found that patients, suddenly used to spending more of their time online because of lockdowns, were generally happy to make the change. For years, telemedicine had been talked about as the coming thing. Now it was here, quickly and spontaneously, and it seemed to be perfectly adequate for a lot of the routine caseload. Many patients liked the lack of waiting and travel time. Doctors recognized the downsides – in particular, the inability to conduct thorough and holistic hands-on examinations – but they could see the benefits, too. In many cases, the most obvious advantage for GP patients was that they could often get a phone or video appointment within hours, rather than days or weeks.

In countries with government-sponsored telephone helplines, many patients were able to access the advice they needed without recourse to the family doctor or the local hospital. Private-sector services came into their own and online information sources like WebMD and specialized apps like Clue, which provides advice about women's health issues, saw record numbers of enquiries. Medical practitioners had long grumbled about the 'Dr Google' phenomenon, which led to many patients jumping to spectacularly unlikely self-diagnoses ("Doctor, doctor, I've got Epstein Barr mononucleosis ... or maybe it's flu!"). But they couldn't help but welcome the trend for patients to take more responsibility for their own wellbeing.

Now that we've seen it in action, it's obvious that various aspects of telemedicine are here to stay. Many people with long-term conditions like diabetes, hypertension, asthma and COPD already have basic monitoring equipment in the home and are actively involved in managing their own health, using prick tests and gadgets like blood pressure monitors, oximeters and spirometers. In the future, most of these are likely to be connected online, giving medical staff real-time information and automatic alerts if something goes wrong.

Good Doctor, one of Ping An's many successful corporate ventures, is essentially an e-commerce platform, reaching out to Chinese consumers and offering, at the first level, free Q&A advice for any medical condition they might have. Patients can then move up to a paid advice scheme, starting with automated triage and then actually talking to an in-house doctor, and finally being referred to wherever is appropriate in the medical system. It's certainly a meaningful value proposition, as evidenced by the company's current valuation of $11 billion, just six years after launch.

Health monitoring technology is moving fast. Some smartwatches can already detect problems like atrial fibrillation or the first signs of a stroke, and many other wearable monitoring devices will be coming onto the market in the next few years. Machine learning systems that can look at video imagery of a mole and warn if it is likely to be an early-stage melanoma are on their way and enthusiasts are already talking about AI-powered scanning mirrors that will pick up on anomalies affecting people's eyes or potentially sinister rashes and skin lesions. There are even mental health monitoring systems in development that can – with a patient's consent – detect the onset of depressive or schizophrenic episodes through real-time recognition of changes in the way the individual talks or writes.

Apart from the benefits to individual patients, online monitoring will also provide a great deal of relevant and structured data which, suitably anonymized, can remove a lot of epidemiological guesswork and be used to refine our understanding of disease transmission. As the coronavirus spread around the world, different countries launched different types of smartphone-based tracking systems – some of them long-range, using GPS, others based on the short-range Bluetooth system. The types of technology used were usually determined by cultural factors and levels of concern about privacy and state surveillance. In Britain, the Covid Symptom Study – a very basic app, with no tracking functionality, that simply invited volunteers to check in every day and report whether they were well or had symptoms – attracted a huge sample base of 4 million users and provided researchers with a mine of useful information.

All this progress in the area of telemedicine is important, in the advanced economies, as a means of improving the efficiency, scope and effectiveness of health systems. But for poorer countries, and those where much of the population is dispersed across remote rural communities, it will be a game changer.

In India, Southeast Asia, Latin America and across Africa, where there are just too few doctors and too many people, the new technologies and innovative services will be the key to bringing proper healthcare to millions of families for the first time. Every doctor subscribes to some version of the Hippocratic Oath, which binds practitioners to work in their patients' interests and to do no harm. But every doctor must also feel the moral imperative to help as many patients as possible. Telemedicine offers new ways of using limited resources more effectively and making a powerful positive impact on the lives of many more people.

"What I see now is a need for business leaders and entrepreneurs to act in a more responsible way, establishing new business models that will be more transparent and rewarding and more productive for a bigger part of society. That's instead of being motivated by creating value just for a limited number of stakeholders – shareholders or managers or people who work for the company. We must try to spread the value created much wider."

DMITRY AKSENOV
CHAIRMAN OF THE BOARD OF DIRECTORS,
RDI GROUP

IT'S AN INTERDEPENDENT WORLD

Winston Churchill once said: "Never let a good crisis go to waste." Well, there's actually no record of Winston saying it, but it's too good a line to ignore. Necessity is the mother of invention, and the Covid-19 catastrophe has certainly galvanized a lot of new thinking about various aspects of both healthcare delivery and climate change.

For Sven Jungmann, whose long training and hands-on experience as a practising doctor in Germany, Brazil and Kenya led, by a somewhat indirect route, to his present involvement in entrepreneurial innovation and advanced medical technologies, the new focus on these two issues comes as no surprise. He has long seen the connections between them, both on the macro level and in his own work.

For example, in the summer of 2018, he was on the front line in Berlin's Emil von Behring Klinik when Europe was hit by a major heatwave. No one could sleep properly, and doctors discarded their white coats and struggled to keep going through long, busy shifts that felt like working in a sauna. Nurses had to put up extra drips to keep their sweltering charges from becoming dehydrated. Many of these people were elderly, suffering from cancer, pneumonia or heart failure and very vulnerable to extreme heat. The doors of the wards were flung open to let the air flow through, as emergency admissions soared and staff throughout the hospital felt they were getting close to their limits.

This was one of the German capital's major hospitals and it was in emergency damage-control mode – hanging on and praying for the weather to change. It was only later that Sven saw the statistics about the global scale of the health problems caused by the heatwave. Altogether, 220 million people had suffered from exposure to the searing heat, beating the previous world record of 209 million, which, itself, had been set just three years earlier, in summer 2015. It was just one more minor milestone on the road towards global warming and climate breakdown.

It's an iron rule in these matters that the poor suffer most. We've seen it, of course, with deaths from Covid-19, even in countries where healthcare is sophisticated and free. In less developed economies, people endure food and water shortages, as well as infectious diseases, in ways that the populations of rich countries do not experience. Half the world's population, roughly 3.5 billion people, still can't benefit from basic health services. Those who can access medical care spend at least 10% of their household budgets on it, driving an estimated 100 million people into extreme poverty.

But we are all interdependent. Transmission between countries was a significant factor in the early days of the coronavirus outbreak, but it was not the only way Covid-19's impact in distant lands affected the big Western economies. Supply chains for foods and manufactured goods were disrupted – and so was the supply of pharmaceuticals from firms in India and China. In recent years, India has become a major supplier of both familiar and specialized drugs, from paracetamol and aspirin to President Trump's favoured hydroxychloroquine. Remdesivir, a failed treatment for hepatitis and Ebola, now licensed in the US as a possible treatment for the new coronavirus, is currently being produced in China, India and even Bangladesh, despite the fact that it is still protected by a patent held by America's Gilead Sciences. Political wrangling between the Indian and Chinese governments, lockdown rules and Covid outbreaks affecting the production centres all have the potential to cut off supplies of many of the drugs the rich world takes for granted.

The multitude of links between countries and continents, and their vulnerability, has encouraged a new spirit of collaboration. Even while they incur eye-watering debts running into trillions of dollars to prop up their own economies, the Western nations are considering plans for big debt relief schemes and cash aid donations to some of the world's poorest countries. These will add even more to the costs of coronavirus, but enlightened self-interest comes into play here. Residual hotspots of infection, after the main flood of Covid-19 recedes, could lead to the re-introduction of the virus and a devastating second wave. It's one world, and aid and debt relief are not just humane initiatives but also, to some extent, an insurance against the nightmare's return.

VALUE-BASED HEALTHCARE PUTS THE PATIENT FRONT AND CENTRE

Innovation in a complex field like health is not always a matter of introducing new drugs, treatments or technologies. Technology often forms part of a new initiative, but its role may be as an enabler, rather than as the star of the show.

In the case of value-based healthcare, an idea that has been gradually gaining momentum since Harvard Professor Michael Porter introduced it in 2007, the innovation lies in the approach, rather than the tools used to deliver it. Everyone's in favour of value-based healthcare, just like everyone's against sin. But the fact that people are still arguing about the nuances of what it implies and struggling to implement it 15 years later actually goes to show what a break it was with previous practice. The essence of it is that outcomes (seen very much from the patient's personal point of view) should be measured, rather than health service outputs (300 inoculations, 15 MRI scans and three appendectomies), and that these should then be related to the costs involved to assess the real value of an intervention.

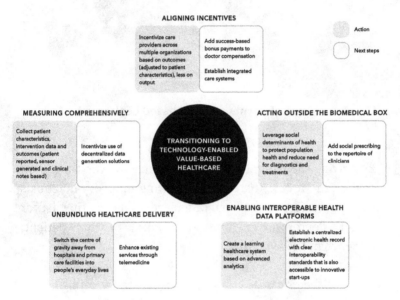

MORE INFORMATION ON WWW.JOINFIGHTBACK.COM

The three pillars of value-based healthcare are personal value (as perceived by the patient), social value (improving health, longevity and quality of life at the population level) and efficiency (better, faster provision at lower cost). Perhaps surprisingly, experience has shown that all three goals can be achieved by a fierce concentration on patients, rather than outputs.

Three elements of value-based healthcare

By putting the patient right at the centre of everything, you change the focus. Instead of following up every diagnosis with a prescription for a pill or a place on the waiting list for surgery, doctors are encouraged to look at the whole patient, rather than the symptom.

If mild diabetes can be brought under control by eating better, walking more and losing a few kilos of weight (the initial target is often a 7% reduction in body weight) as effectively as with metformin tablets or even injectable insulin, this is better all round. It's better for the patient, who becomes generally healthier, avoids side-effects and will be more resistant to infectious disease. It costs the healthcare provider less, leaving more resources for essentials like kidney transplants, cataract operations, mental health services and maternity care. Importantly, it also gives the individual an empowering sense of agency. Feeling that you are involved in managing your own health has been shown to be a benefit in itself for many patients.

In the face of today's biggest challenges – Covid-19 in the last few months, climate change in the next few years – value-based healthcare points us towards investing in building a more resilient society, with fitter citizens and better individual and population resistance to stress and disease. This means encouraging and aiding people to make better lifestyle choices about diet, alcohol, smoking, exercise and owning dogs, which will help them avoid preventable diseases and maintain good mental health. This makes individuals – and society – less vulnerable to the assaults of pandemics, heatwaves and other shocks. It also minimizes avoidable hospital treatment, leaving a margin of surge capacity in the system for unexpected crises.

But all the smart thinking that's gone into this slow-burning value-based healthcare revolution tends to lead to the conclusion that only the right technologies can capture the data needed to turn the good intentions into realities. Value-based healthcare relies on accurate information, including the patients' subjective opinions about outcomes and real-time data collected from sensors, mobile devices and online monitoring and warning systems. It also depends on good data analytics and sensible comparisons across different hospitals and regions to highlight instances of erratic performance and poor value for money.

In the UK's National Health Service, for example, consolidated data from England's 135 Clinical Commissioning Groups revealed that some parts of the country used diagnostic CT scans nearly five times as often, per thousand patients, as others. As the report that uncovered this huge variation commented drily: "It is currently not clear what the level of CT activity for a population *should* be, but both underuse and overuse of CT scanning could be harmful to patients (high doses of radiation are associated with CT scanning)." One NHS review claimed that just reducing this kind of "unwarranted variation" could save at least 9% of the £55.6 billion ($68 billion) spent by Britain's acute care hospitals every year.

In the long run, value-based healthcare will not be just for the world's richer nations. In places where the need for medical and health services far outstrips a country's ability to provide adequate funding or staffing, this approach can help the development of policies based on real-world evidence. Once implemented, it will make it easier to lower costs and improve outcomes by cutting over-prescribing and establishing standardized treatments for specific diseases, in line with local conditions and preferences. Many low- and middle-income countries, such as South Africa and Nigeria, still lack the underlying systems and technologies – elements like disease registries and electronic patient records – that are needed to underpin the shift away from the more traditional output-based approach. But some others are making impressive progress. Countries like Turkey and Colombia have adopted national value-based healthcare plans and are now moving towards patient-centred systems that can deliver cost-effective results while pushing services out into rural areas and giving individualized treatment to large numbers of people.

IT'S NOT OUR LITTLE LOCAL DIFFICULTY

If a patient-centred approach is best for sick people, could something similar be put into practice for an ailing planet? Clearly not, if we can't develop a less fragmented and more holistic view of our world and the threats it faces. Our track record so far is not impressive.

If it would take Covid-style lockdowns for several months every single year to reduce carbon emissions to the targets set in the 2015 Paris Agreement, the one thing we can be sure of is that that's not going to happen. Instead, we need vast, coordinated, costly, collaborative action, on many different fronts and on a worldwide scale.

There is, as always, a fatal tendency for different countries and constituencies to focus on the parts of the picture that seem immediately relevant to their interests. Island states and low-lying countries, like Bangladesh and the Netherlands, are urgently concerned about rising sea levels. Australia, Sweden, California and even parts of Northern Siberia, above the Arctic Circle, are seared by uncontrollable wildfires. The US and the Caribbean nations feel the impact of ever more powerful hurricanes. German and British towns are flooded every year.

At the end of 2019, a report by Christian Aid totted up the crude cost of 15 of the year's worst climate-related disasters. The totals came to more than 4,500 deaths and $140 billion-worth of damage. Both figures are certain to be underestimates.

Climate change and pollution are combining to accelerate the loss of biodiversity, depleting the ecosystems that make life on Earth possible. That sounds like one of the more subtle consequences of the global problem. But it's not, when you start to look at what it will mean in practical terms. The honey bees that buzz around our gardens in summer are under threat from habitat loss, new diseases, pesticides and changes in land use. But bees don't just make honey for us. They pollinate food crops as well. And if the bees go, we are in deep trouble. In 2020, three-quarters of Europe's food production depends on bee pollination.

We are just beginning, as humans, to realize how interdependent we are, across borders and across continents. We haven't even begun to recognize and acknowledge the extent of our cross-species interdependencies. The bees need us to make changes to keep them alive and thriving. We need them and their work, just to keep us going.

And we don't need a plague of locusts. Spring 2020 saw the greatest swarms of locusts for 70 years, darkening the sky and stripping fields bare of food and cash crops right across East Africa and the Middle East, and into Pakistan and India. This biblical plague, which last appeared as a major problem in 2005, has resurfaced as a result of shifting weather patterns caused by climate change. Locust swarms can be terrifyingly efficient. Each day, a modest swarm of 40 million can eat as much as 35,000 people, while a big one can include up to 70 billion insects. The locusts, a form of grasshopper, will quickly devour cotton, wheat, onions, mustard, chilli peppers – virtually anything that grows – leaving starvation and economic devastation in their wake. Pakistan, suffering cruelly as Covid-19 races through the population, declared the locust swarms a national emergency. In May, the World Bank launched a $500 million programme to help people in the 23 countries worst hit by the invasion from the skies.

DIGITAL FOR THE CLIMATE

Thank you for bearing with us. You may have been wondering why we've spent so many pages skirting around the elephant in the room: how much relevance does all this have to the Fourth Industrial Revolution and platform strategies?

The answer is 15%. That's how much could potentially be saved, just by digitizing today's industries with current technologies. Here's an overview:

ENERGY SUPPLY

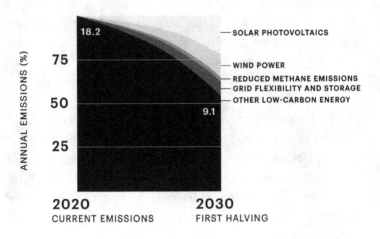

TRANSPORT

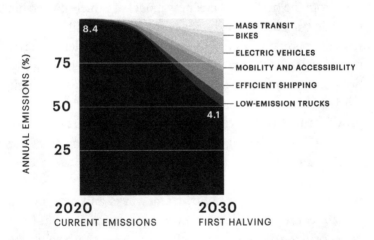

MORE INFORMATION ON WWW.JOINFIGHTBACK.COM
ADAPTED FROM GLOBAL CLIMATE ACTION SUMMIT

What you are seeing here, looking at transport, for example, is the contribution that digital technologies could have on the overall goal of reducing global emissions by 50%. Some estimates put the figure for transport's contribution to global emissions as high as 21%, with almost three-quarters of that coming from short journeys.

Several technologies are now converging that will ensure the transport sector undergoes its most dramatic transformation in a century. In the last two years, every major car and truck manufacturer has announced electrification plans. In China, Shenzhen's fleet of 16,000 buses is completely electric and the city's taxis will soon follow.

But the real game changer will be electric and driverless cars and trucks. 5G is a pivotal technology for safety, efficiency and reliability in this context. Driverless vehicles will accelerate a shift from the traditional business model of vehicle ownership towards transport as a service. Fewer people will own cars. Instead, people will take shared rides in driverless electric taxis – which, of course, can operate tirelessly, 24 hours a day, bringing operating costs and fares right down – or catching a driverless bus. As our recent lockdown experiences have proved, there is also the potential for greater use of video calls and homeworking to remove the need for much of our routine travel.

In fact, with the right policy frameworks and determined climate-conscious leadership, every industry can benefit from our continuously improving technology. Smart tech solutions will be instrumental in moving society towards a circular and lean economy, focused on growing service value while reducing waste and pollution, potentially by far more than the 15% we might target today.

The world's response to the ultimate challenge of climate breakdown needs to operate on many different levels. Government policies and priorities need to change, but so do the actions and habits of consumers and the businesses that supply their wants and needs. In the end, big, permanent changes can only be made when people have options and alternatives that encourage them to willingly modify their patterns of consumption.

It's obvious, though, that many of the enterprising start-ups that couple idealistic notions of saving the world with the aim of becoming profitable businesses will fail. Sometimes, even an attractive idea doesn't quite meet a market need. Sometimes, all it takes is time, technology and a slight realignment of people's assumptions about what is possible.

One New York-based company, Bowery Farming, is using robotics, sophisticated proprietary software and LED lights to grow vegetables in warehouse farms in the middle of the Big Apple, using 95% less water than conventional agriculture. A new business, Solytic, that we have been involved in launching with a major energy company, Vattenfall, is deploying smart AI systems to squeeze productivity increases of up to 30% out of photovoltaic solar panel arrays. Blockchain techniques are being used to make supply chains fully transparent, cut out waste and corruption and balance supply and demand. And 3D printing is beginning to prove its value for specialized short-run manufacturing – not just because of its ability to handle unmouldable shapes, but also because it leaves behind no offcuts and wasted materials.

MOVING TOWARDS A CIRCULAR ECONOMY

One huge opportunity to reduce waste and environmental impact is the idea of the Circular Economy. Philosophically pleasing and practically hard to achieve, it is a concept that has been around for centuries but is being helped to fruition by the new technologies we have available to us.

There are now plenty of examples in the waste management industry, where internet-connected sensors, AI, optical recognition devices and robot systems are helping to pick through streams of waste, extract the usable items and turn garbage into raw materials, converting outputs from one process into inputs for the next. We'll soon have 5G-equipped scanning drones adding another dimension to these activities. But the trick, as always, is to find ways of performing this modern alchemy profitably and on a large scale. Paper has been recycled since the 19th century, and two-thirds of all the paper used in the West now comes from recovered materials. Two-fifths of our copper, one-third of our glass and half of our aluminium comes from recycling streams. Progress is being made with the recycling of electronic and electrical goods, but plastics are still a major problem – only 10% can currently be reused.

If we have the will and the creativity, there are few limits to the challenges we can set for ourselves. Energy-intensive Alphabet is fully powered by renewables. Unilever already has 26 brands that are 100% sustainably sourced from agricultural raw materials. Daimler aims to be completely carbon-neutral by 2039, sourcing 3,000 to 5,000 components from around the world without creating any net emissions.

Toyota is mounting a major drive towards more hybrid, electric and fuel-cell cars and trucks. So the manufacturers are moving in the right direction, but consumers may sometimes need nudging. When we talked to Alain Uyttenhoven, President of Toyota Germany, he was frank about the need for a stick-and-carrot approach: "We have to reinvent our mobility ecosystem by incentivizing the right choices. And we have to reinvent it in a way that has rewards and a little bit of punishment, maybe 90% stick, 10% carrot. The choices we make as a society should reflect our hopes, not our fears."

We would hardly have imagined the CEO of a world-leading food company arguing that "the food system we've built over the last century is a dead end for the future". But the CEO of Danone, Emmanuel Faber, has recently come out and said just that. Danone is now working to develop and promote regenerative models for its agricultural suppliers.

Then there are the investors. Sustainable investing has accelerated to such an extent that it's now part of the mainstream. The most prominent example here is Blackrock, the world's largest asset management company. It has declared its intention to divest from fossil fuel investments entirely and says that sustainable investment will form the foundation of future client portfolios.

Environmental activist, Arctic explorer and author Sebastian Copeland sums up the changing attitudes to recycling with a shrewdly realistic eye.

"We need hybrid models that can help save the environment while creating sustainable and stable businesses," he says. "In the past, you had the Greenpeace guys – super-passionate, but no business brains – and the business guys, who were only looking at the bottom line. Now the two sides are moving together to build a new species of hybrid start-up."

With enough ingenuity and big enough incentives, almost everything can potentially be recycled and the Circular Economy can become a reality. We have the opportunity to move beyond traditional linear industry models and the 'take – make – waste' economy we inherited from the original Industrial Revolution.

We could design out waste, so we used less of the world's finite raw materials. We could make a shift away from planned obsolescence and produce repairable consumer goods, so that household items did not have to be thrown away the moment something went wrong. And we could rethink our consumption models so that manufacturers had real cash incentives to make long-lasting, efficient products. For the last five years, all the lights at Amsterdam's Schiphol Airport have been provided by Philips on a lighting-as-a-service contract that turns the usual business model on its head. Philips used to make money by selling the airport light bulbs. Every time a bulb failed, Philips made a profit. Under the fixed-cost lighting-as-a-service model, it is absolutely in the company's interests to keep its manufacturing and maintenance costs down by supplying light bulbs that go on for ever.

The world is full of opportunities to apply Circular Economy principles, but the Dutch seem to have developed a talent for this kind of lateral eco-thinking. A company in Amsterdam has recently begun marketing trainers with soles made entirely from chewing gum scraped up from the city's streets. That's only possible because plastic polymers can be chemically unwound into their original hydrocarbon chains. But it's a good example of the problems that need to be overcome. You can't buck the laws of economics, and hundreds of everyday polymers can be churned out from petrochemical feedstocks at incredibly low prices. There may be environmental and social reasons to recycle, but there is no cash incentive. Recycled materials compete with virgin materials, so the recyclers tend to be hostages to volatile raw material prices. What adds up one day can come crashing down when commodity prices fluctuate. The recyclers' costs depend on the cost of collecting, distributing and processing scrap, which tend to be stable, while world commodity prices, which determine how much recyclers can get for their materials, can be extremely volatile. If prices for primary resources crash, recovered materials are no longer competitive and recyclers can quickly go out of business. As Professor Rita McGrath said, earlier in this book, the externalities are just not priced into the costs of the raw materials.

This economic fragility makes the long-term investment that's needed for a high-technology recycling plant precarious, even illogical, and it tends to keep most recycling businesses small and inefficient. This, in turn, constrains their ability to guarantee a steady and predictable supply of recovered materials, which is what big manufacturers demand.

It's a chicken and egg problem, and one that needs to be solved if the Circular Economy is to become something more than an enticing theory. Scale is what's needed. Once scale and stability are achieved, the boot's on the other foot, as recyclers can potentially leverage powerful economies of scale. That's where it all started, with paper recycling 150 years ago. There was so much paper available that prices didn't swing up and down, recovery was able to happen on a large scale and the paper recycling businesses could afford the investment they needed to work efficiently.

However, you can get round the scale problem, as some smaller start-ups are proving. Anna Alex, co-founder of Planetly, and previously founder of online fashion company Outfittery, has just raised €5.2 million in her first funding round in pursuit of Planetly's vision to be the most actionable tool to fight the climate crisis, based on automated data collection and analysis.

There is money in this. According to leading Circular Economy authority Ellen MacArthur, this green trend is turning into a hard-edged business opportunity that will be worth $1 trillion by 2025 and $4.5 trillion in the following decade. The European Green Deal certainly supports that notion, and there are forecasts that it will not only create massive environmental benefits but also 700,000 new jobs by 2030.

Circularity has another advantage, too, in that it makes companies and governments less reliant on international supply chains. Covid-19 proved these chains to be weaker than people had hoped, and more vulnerable to disruptions, affecting production, storage, consumption and waste management. As companies and countries get to rely more and more on their own ability to produce, distribute, recycle and discharge, they are increasing their resilience in the face of sudden shocks.

A lot of potentially climate-friendly behaviour doesn't yet happen at scale because the green alternatives are too inconvenient or too expensive. Data-driven business models can create clarity around these issues, simplifying choices and facilitating planet-friendly options.

Steven Tebbe is MD of CDP, an international nonprofit that helps companies and states measure the environmental impact of their activities. He believes accurate measurement and full disclosure are vital in this area. "There are very clear, very tangible business benefits in terms of companies understanding where they are, where their risks and opportunities are, and benchmarking themselves," he says. "Disclosure and transparency must be the first step in taking any action."

His colleague, Laurent Babikian, puts the CDP initiative into perspective: "It took time to create standards for financial data and it's taking time to create standards for non-financial data. But crises like Covid-19 will accelerate the implementation of these standards. The more we see that climate change is a huge threat to long-term value creation for investors, the faster this will come to the market."

Better data means better decisions. And with new technologies come new realities that give rise to new forms of circularity. Roland Deiser, Director of the Center for the Future of Organization at the Drucker School of Management, sees many of our traditional assumptions being turned on their heads. Cars, for example, may shed their gas-guzzling past and become net contributors to the energy economy. "The electrification of cars puts pressure on the grid," says Deiser. "But there are cars out there that could become mini power plants or storage units and create a completely new paradigm of distributed energy production and distribution. That creates an ecosystem dynamic, because we were looking at energy as one thing and the car as another, and suddenly there's an interplay between them."

Throughout this section, you will have seen two key messages running through nearly every paragraph. First, there is a real urgency for us to act on many different fronts to protect our lives and livelihoods. Secondly, there are tremendous business opportunities up for grabs in these emerging industries.

The difference now, though, is that, because of their complexity, these challenges are harder to conquer than almost any other challenge humanity has faced. At the same time, we have possibilities at our fingertips that were unthinkable even 20 years ago. But to mobilize them and change our world, we need to first adapt our approaches to creating new solutions.

As Bertelsmann's Brigitte Mohn puts it: "The VC approach and the fragmented use of equity within Europe for the promotion of innovation, aimed at transforming and developing industries and societies are not enough. We need an integrated approach that goes beyond asset classes, technologies, geographies and industries. The central objective must be to create businesses that are resilient and regenerative and portfolios that focus on impact and outcomes."

What we need, as you will read in Section 5, is a new and different kind of asset class, corporate venture building, that is better suited to these impact-driven and science-based solutions. The complexity of the challenges requires us to contribute to one another and learn from one another as we unite towards a common purpose. Given the interdependence that characterizes our ecosystem, the success of individuals and businesses will be dictated by their ability to make the right connections within the relevant ecosystems.

As business leaders think about defining the new normal, they will have to consider both the short-term and long-term economic and social effects of their strategic decisions. They'll also need to determine whether or not their solutions contribute to structural change for more social or planetary resilience, as illustrated in the following Venn diagram (inspired by Michael G. Jacobides and Martin Reeves).

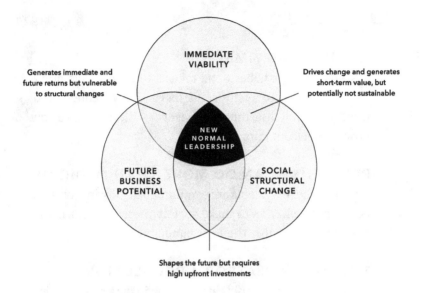

Generates immediate and
future returns but vulnerable
to structural changes

IMMEDIATE
VIABILITY

Drives change and generates
short-term value, but
potentially not sustainable

NEW
NORMAL
LEADERSHIP

FUTURE
BUSINESS
POTENTIAL

SOCIAL
STRUCTURAL
CHANGE

Shapes the future but requires
high upfront investments

And, by the way, if you are looking for strategic inspiration, the UN's 17 Sustainable Development Goals – covering the big global issues like poverty, hunger, disease, sanitation and schooling – might provide some useful clues to guide your search for solutions that hold the promise of a better future.

But before we move on to the necessary structural changes and to corporate venture building as a new asset class, there's one more thing we need to explore. It's the smallest and most important part of the whole movement.

It's you – and your fellow creators.

KEY CONCEPTS

1. **IT'S NO-TIME TIME**
   Systemic change is hard and takes a long time. We don't have that time. To avoid facing increasingly frequent and intense natural disasters, we must act with full dedication now to meet our climate goals.

2. **RESILIENCE CAN DO MORE THAN MEDICINE**
   Most healthcare systems are overburdened. Moving towards better public health to make society more resilient is the best defence against the next pandemic.

3. **THE OTHER PLATFORM REVOLUTION**
   Platform business models are drafting in data technologies from e-commerce, fintech and social media to get to grips with healthcare and climate problems.

OUR KEY RECOMMENDATIONS FOR YOU:

- Leaders must work to make the planet and its inhabitants healthier. It's a moral obligation, and you don't need to be a healthcare company to do it. Apart from anything else, health outcomes depend more on people's diet, education, income and social life than they do on the healthcare system.

- Leadership in the new normal must focus on three strategic goals – staying viable in the short term, shaping the business to ensure a sustainable future and contributing to the structural changes that will help build a better society. That'll mean finding new ways to make the most of every available asset.

- Don't just work on reducing your company's carbon footprint. Aim to develop technologies and business models that change the system and make it more sustainable. Let the UN's Sustainable Development Goals be your inspiration.

- Human resilience depends on healthy populations. We have the technologies to handle major emergencies and make everybody's health better. Your own company has underused assets you could be leveraging to help people lead healthier lives and adapt faster to change.

- Survival is not something you can put on the back burner. The clock is ticking for our climate, oceans and habitats. If we don't invest massively now, we'll be leaving a nightmare for our children and grandchildren. Covid-19 was just a foretaste of what's heading our way.

'WE NEED TO FIND OUR GRETA THUNBERG'

It's one thing to create a company; it's another to create a whole industry. Ida Tin has done both. She is also credited with launching the term 'femtech' for technology that addresses women's biological needs. The femtech sector is expected to be worth $50 billion by 2025. Tin is also the co-founder and CEO of Clue, a women's health app with 12 million users in 190 countries. She's an adventurer at heart and an entrepreneur by destiny, and her trailblazing journey has made her a role model for the next generation of female entrepreneurs.

Some people are born to be pioneers. When she was less than two years old, Tin's Danish parents wrote a book called *Good Luck: By Motorcycle with Emil and Ida Through South America*. It told of their exploits, in and out of the saddle, with two tiny children, in the Andes, the Amazon and the Pampas.

Twenty-four years later, she founded a motorcycle adventure touring company, in partnership with her father, which ran for five years. She's also had her own jewellery company. What she hasn't had is a job. "Well," she admits, "I've actually had two jobs, but I got fired from both within a week." One of them was with KPMG, which quickly decided she didn't fit in because she "didn't have the corporate mindset".

So she was always destined to be an entrepreneur. And since 2013, she's been a very high-profile one, as the co-founder, CEO and public face of Clue, a revolutionary, science-based mobile app for women that tracks their periods and female health more broadly.

Clue has more than 12 million active users and is growing fast in virtually every country in the world. It has raised $30 million in venture capital funding and is a global leader in femtech, a term Ida Tin coined on the spur of the moment ahead of a TechCrunch conference in 2016.

"Everyone was familiar with the idea of fintech and I just thought we needed a word that described technology that was being used to support female health. 'Femtech' seemed like a very natural label for this new category."

Clue stemmed directly from Tin's own need for something that would help her avoid getting pregnant. She was aware of the potential of the smartphone and she was hoping to find an innovation that could be turned into a product, but nothing seemed to be available.

"I'd been travelling around the world with my parents since I was a baby and I'd seen the global need for women to be able to take control of their childbearing," she says. "I thought we must be able to do something that was data-driven, using the phone as the interface to the user. Technology had to be able to play a role."

She's not a techie, but she had two brothers who were programmers and she'd always been around technology. She'd been the proud owner of the very first laptop Apple produced and she'd had every subsequent model.

She was always interested in business, though, and her entrepreneurial potential was nurtured at Denmark's 'alternative business school', Kaospilot, in Aarhus.

When she finished her studies, she formed Moto Mundo and led two-wheel tours to Mongolia, Chile, Vietnam and other exotic destinations until the time came for her to start thinking about having children. She stopped biking to far-flung lands, but her restless spirit was soon ready for the next challenge and her thoughts turned to how the new digital technologies could be harnessed to produce much-needed innovations in women's health.

"My first idea was that I wanted to build a home diagnostics kit that would measure the hormones in your saliva," she says. "That would revolutionize family planning. We tried to do it for four years, but we didn't have the right partners or resources. I kept asking people, 'Why is the technology for this not emerging?' and the answer I got back was usually just the same: 'Well, the people in charge are men, and they probably don't think about it much.'

"Family planning is arguably one of the biggest use cases there is. It determines the future of the planet, and the opportunity is huge. But how can there be such a blind spot? I find it infuriating."

The aim is for Clue to become a brand for female health that's trusted around the world, helping people understand their bodies and find the advice and services they need. The app is scrupulously science-based and fact-checked. But it's not girly, like Goop, actress Gwyneth Paltrow's female lifestyle brand, or coldly clinical.

"Women need something that's as scientifically valid as WebMD, but that talks to them in a language that's not condescending or pinkified," she says.

"I want to create a cultural shift and provide a voice for women. We need to open everyone's eyes to how central this part of life is, for half the world's population, and how much it shapes people's lives.

"In India today there are women having their wombs removed so they won't have periods and can work in the fields every day of the month. And there are so many questions. Why do people have cramps? We don't really know. Why do we have hot flushes? We don't know. When am I ovulating? In some countries, the big question is 'Can I still cook when I'm having my period?'"

Technology, she says, has to serve people and serve the planet. "If everything's measured solely by revenues and profits "we're going to end up in bad places."

Clue is starting to develop ways of monetizing its success, but it is never going to be about making money for its own sake. It won't feature advertisements in the app and it won't sell the data it collects, though it is freely sharing anonymized information with carefully selected research partners, including teams at Stanford, Columbia and Oxford universities.

Providing information is Clue's primary purpose, but Tin is proud of some of the technological breakthroughs her 70-person team has come up with.

"We've built an AI product that's super cool, that can help people understand if they have a common condition known as PCOS — polycystic ovary syndrome. There's so much we could do, but every little step helps."

Innovation is vital, but Tin sees a lot more talk than action. When she meets with groups of business leaders, she hears them talk about innovation and fighting back against the ruthless American and Chinese companies that threaten to dominate the digital world.

"But there is so much fear in these rooms," she says. "There's fear, conservatism and complacency, and people don't know what to do. There seems to be this idea that says: 'Oh, AI is coming. Maybe some jobs are going to change. But maybe the Americans are just much better than us at building unicorns.' We need to get people out of their half-asleep, half fear-frozen condition.

"We need really good VCs who know how to build companies, who aren't going to ask early-stage start-ups for their five-year revenue projections. That just kills them."

The big change that would see Europe up its game and start successfully using technology to create a better future for everyone is cultural, rather than technological. The FightBack campaign is a good start, she says, "a heroic initiative" that could help to set the ball rolling.

"Maybe we need to come up with a really good hash-tag, like 2014's ice-bucket challenge, to grab people's attention," she says.

Technology, she believes, should be a force for good in the world, and Europe should be taking the lead. The aim should be to build technologies that enhance our humanity, rather than adding to the levels of alienation, addiction and disengagement in society.

"We need to find leaders with vision and courage and absolute clarity, who can inspire a mass movement. We need to find our Malala, or our Greta Thunberg. We need to hear them and amplify their voices.

"What got us here is not going to get us out of here. And we got here with a very one-sided, gendered approach. We need something that sees more. And we need much more diverse eyes to look, or we won't see what we need to see."

TIME TO MAKE GOING GREEN PAY

"People don't do that." We can't possibly know how many founders hear this when they first pitch their start-up ideas. What we can say, for certain, is that only a special few manage to turn the status quo on its head. Brian Chesky and his co-founders have done it with Airbnb, convincing people it's OK to stay in strangers' houses. Nicolas Brusson, CEO of BlaBlaCar, and his co-founders have done it, too, making it quite normal to hop into a car with total strangers and drive hundreds of miles. BlaBlaCar is one of France's top unicorn start-ups and the world's largest long-distance carpooling service, boasting around 65 million users across 22 countries. It's safe to say, this is a game that's been changed. People do do that now.

Back in 2007, a little start-up company based at Cornell University, in New York State, started offering a carpooling service, mainly to students, that matched car drivers with empty seats with passengers looking to travel. The company, Zimride, grew but never fulfilled its initial promise. Eventually, the owners decided to pivot and put their effort behind a subsidiary. That subsidiary was called Lyft, and you know where the story goes from there.

Meanwhile – or, if anything, slightly earlier – on the other side of the Atlantic, three young Frenchmen, based in Paris, were also trying to develop the idea of carpooling.

BlaBlaCar has stuck to its guns, though, and resisted the temptation to cross over into what is now known as the ridesharing market to fight it out with Uber and Lyft. Instead, it has stayed with its original idea, focusing mainly on long-distance journeys (average distance is 263 km) and expanding steadily into 22 countries. With a market valuation of around $1.6 billion, it is one of the small handful of high-tech unicorns created in France.

Nicolas Brusson, BlaBlaCar's CEO, was one of the original founding trio. The three of them all shared a strong streak of idealism and it still burns bright in Brusson as he contemplates the future of our relationship with the motor car.

"The car is the best and most disruptive invention we've had in the last 100 years," he says. "But mobility accounts for more than 10% of all global CO_2 emissions.

"In the next ten to 20 years, our use of the car is going to have to change completely. Cars are 80% empty. The car must evolve from an object you buy into something you just use, with some model of shared mobility, like carpooling or car-sharing."

He sees the amount of energy we use to drive empty seats around as absurd. BlaBlaCar is doing something towards increasing efficiency, saving 1.6 million tonnes of CO_2 every year, the equivalent of the entire transport emissions of a city like Paris. But even that is only a drop in the ocean compared with the broader problem of climate change. The climate emergency needs to be tackled from many different angles, he says, and that need is also about to create a wealth of attractive and profitable opportunities for entrepreneurs.

"If I were starting a new company today, I'd really try to find an idea that would help to address some aspect of global warming. A lot of funding will be going into companies like that over the next few years, and I think regulations are probably going to be relaxed to help them grow quickly."

That would certainly be a way of bringing the profit motive into play, alongside well-meaning altruism, and signalling to the market that entrepreneurial ideas to help ward off a climate disaster would be welcomed and rewarded.

On the subject of regulation, however, Brusson is not impressed by the way our governments operate at the moment.

He believes Europe could be doing more, within the rules of international trade, to make it easier for home-grown entrepreneurs to start and scale new businesses. It might even, he thinks, be possible to make life slightly harder for the non-European giants, which have proved adept at finding ways to play the system, including taking advantage of local rules to benefit from locating various operations in Ireland.

"It's a strategic issue for Europe. We've been naïve. We've made it very easy for the US and Chinese companies to go and win in Europe."

As BlaBlaCar has expanded across the continent, it has run up against unhelpful regulations that define carpooling differently in France, Germany, the UK, Spain and other countries and impose different rules about, say, the minimum or maximum amount the driver can collect from the passenger. The lack of harmonization, in this and other fields, fragments the European market and doesn't help indigenous companies grow fast to reach critical mass.

"Europe has done well in terms of unicorns and funding rounds in the last few years," says Brusson. "But we are still very far behind when it comes to scaling platforms and digital companies. The gap between Europe and the US and China has widened even more.

"We have Spotify, but we don't have the giants. But we have a nice cohort now of fintechs, like N26 and Revolut. If we had harmonized regulations, it would help those guys become super big in a European market of 400 million or 500 million people and then go on to expand in other markets in the world."

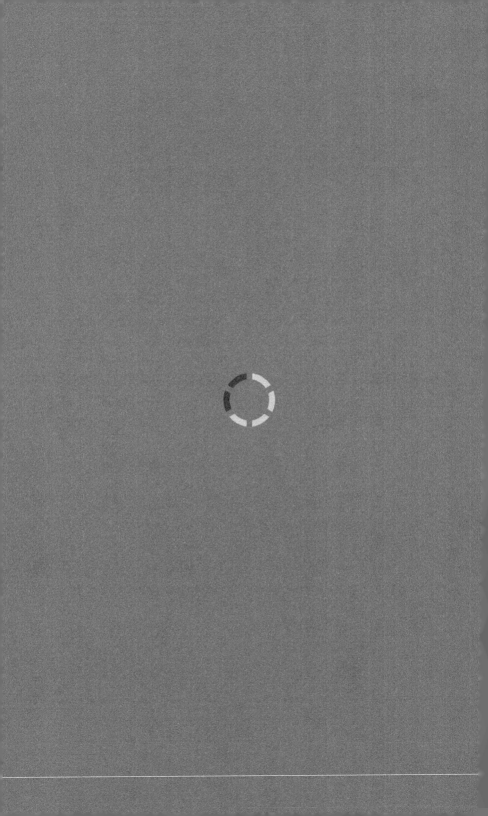

SECTION 4

HELPING LEADERS TUNE IN TO THE ENTREPRENEURIAL MINDSET

THE YEAR OF THE EVERYDAY ENTREPRENEURS

One of the most heartening and inspiring aspects of the reaction to 2020's coronavirus pandemic was the sudden rise of the everyday entrepreneur.

Ordinary people – or extraordinary people who hadn't quite known what they were capable of – grabbed the initiative and made good things happen. Stay-at-home mums started little local Facebook groups to make sure elderly neighbours got their food and medicines, and found themselves marshalling informal supply services for hundreds of people. An English garage worker who occasionally ran pub quizzes decided to do some online to raise money for health service charities and set a new world record for a live online quiz, attracting 182,000 participants. Yoga groups and poetry circles that decided to sew a few facemasks for nursing homes and clinics soon turned into busy cooperatives with hundreds of voluntary workers and a vital role to play in plugging gaps in the supply chain. Countless hackathons, mostly run remotely, gave birth to unusual solutions for everything from domestic violence to infection tracking.

This was entrepreneurial activity in a very pure, elemental form, uncontaminated by money, ambition or other external motivations. People did what they did for their own internal reasons. They got on with solving the immediate problems they could see in front of them, without asking anyone's permission or authorization and usually without the expectation of any reward at all, other than the feeling that they were doing what was right. When a few of the most exceptional cases attracted media attention, the everyday entrepreneurs who found themselves in front of the microphones often found it hard to say what had prompted them to act. "Somebody had to do it, so I thought I'd better get on with it," one London grandmother told the BBC.

Four types of entrepreneur

A much younger woman, a student who had spontaneously organized a network of volunteers to make regular friendship calls to isolated pensioners, summed up the spirit that drove so many of these improvised initiatives. "I wanted to make a difference," she said. "Covid's so horrible, and so many people were suffering at home, in hospitals or in care homes. I couldn't watch Netflix all day and sit there in my flat doing nothing."

This desire to make a difference – Sven likes to quote Steve Jobs's inspirational line about "making a dent in the universe" – is not something everyone shares. We have all seen ample evidence of it among the high-profile entrepreneurs who have founded so many influential global businesses over the last 20 years, but there are many other people who, quite understandably, prefer a quieter life of structure, order and reasonable predictability.

What the coronavirus catastrophe has demonstrated, though, is that there is an inventive, innovative streak that is latent in many individuals – across all countries, industries, generations and classes – who have never really found the opportunities to exercise it. This energetic creative spirit is an asset we have tended to overlook, perhaps because we have been hypnotized by the popular myth of the 'hero entrepreneur'. The fact is that there are a lot more people with entrepreneurial talents in any company, any town, any society, than we have generally recognized. In the aftermath of the greatest shock to the system since World War II, we will need all the help we can get to rebuild our lives and our economies. Leveraging the undervalued potential of this pool of everyday entrepreneurs – and of those who have been inspired by their example – is going to play a big part in the recovery.

'Build back better' is a slogan that has been around for a few years, since it was first aired at the UN's 2015 World Conference on Disaster Risk Reduction in Sendai, Japan. It was originally seen as a rousing call to arms that would provide a useful touchstone for those involved in recovery and reconstruction work after natural disasters like floods and hurricanes, mainly in the developing world. But it is equally applicable to the rebuilding and investment programmes that are being put in place everywhere as the recovery from Covid-19 gets under way.

Simply reinstating what we had before and returning to business as usual will not be possible or desirable, especially as the world slides towards the cliff edge of irreversible climate change. We need to make our rebuilt societies better, healthier, more resilient, more equitable and more sustainable. We will need all the energy and ideas we can get our hands on, and we will need our entrepreneurs to make a massive contribution.

INNOVATORS ON THE INSIDE

All companies are born as start-ups, but some of them go on to become behemoths. Even in their adult years, they can still be entrepreneurial, though they're made up of people and their actions can only ever reflect the ingenuity and dynamism of the people they have on the payroll. Sometimes they don't even know what they've got going for them until a crisis fires them up and gets them thinking along new and unexpected lines.

As Geoffrey Parker, research fellow and visiting scholar at MIT's Initiative for the Digital Economy, points out, the coronavirus pandemic has ignited inventive energies in companies that they didn't know they had.

"Hewlett-Packard used to make printers; now they make face masks," he says. "It's a cool story, but it's a story on a small scale. The real question is, 'How can they make that a story on a large scale?' Because, those were assets they had that they were able to quickly redeploy.

"Why isn't that the way these firms always interoperate and cooperate? Why does it take Covid-19 and a complete shutdown of commerce to get that obvious efficiency gain?"

Linda Hill saw much the same kind of galvanizing effect at work in a global healthcare company. As an eminent professor at Harvard Business School, she's used to looking closely at what happens inside big companies. What she observed in one particular study was the way the sudden pressure from Covid-19 led to the decentralization of entrepreneurial activity, so that it spread out beyond the departments normally charged with coming up with new ideas.

"The leadership began to emphasize that innovation can be done by everyone," she told us. "This unleashed innovative solutions from people throughout the organization at all levels, many critical to their response to Covid." In one regional supermarket chain, the CEO commented that the coronavirus crisis had revealed just how much latent potential there was in the organization, as individuals who had never been viewed as leaders volunteered to address some of the most difficult challenges the company faced.

So does every organization have this capacity to find previously unrecognized entrepreneurial talents within its ranks when the going gets tough?

Not necessarily. But many can. There are a lot of corporations where mould-breaking initiative is routinely undervalued, perhaps even discouraged by a web of KPIs and siloed departmental structures and procedures. Individuals who are not incentivized to flex their entrepreneurial muscles may not even realize what they could be capable of.

Practice makes perfect, as we know. There's a classic golfer's saying, first popularized by Lee Trevino in 1969: "The more I practise, the luckier I get." Trevino was a golfing legend and a smart guy, though he'd left school at 14. He knew that the way to become expert at anything is to do it often. Repressed entrepreneurs may conveniently emerge from the shadows when their employers need them, but it makes much more sense to give them some scope to develop and practise their talents before there's a desperate need for them. Organizations that want to find the entrepreneurs within should provide opportunities for those people with a flair for thinking up innovative solutions to argue for and implement new ideas as a regular part of their career development.

IT'S A DIFFERENT WAY OF THINKING

So it's not true that entrepreneurs are some special, unique breed, blessed by the gods with inborn superpowers. But there are certain identifiable attributes, traits and tendencies that many of them share. It's worth looking at these in some detail, because there are also a lot of unhelpful myths that need putting to bed. At the same time, it's clear that those who self-identify as entrepreneurs tend to have some particular prejudices and proclivities that are genuinely a little different from those of people who've chosen a more familiar career path.

Not surprisingly, entrepreneurs are often reluctant to work within those established organizations that may be hoping to capture the full force of their drive and expertise through mechanisms like incubators and accelerator programmes, or simply by acquiring the start-ups they've created.

The truth is, these people – the out-and-out, full-time entrepreneurs who see that as their life's mission – don't think quite like everybody else does. Their motivation is often unlike other people's, and their attitudes to risk and reward are sometimes unimaginably different. When contemplating collaborative ventures between large, established organizations and individuals like this, you need to know what you're dealing with.

Alex Manson, Singapore-based head of Standard Chartered's SC Ventures, has seen the problems and knows the kind of adjustments senior executives may need to make. The corporate disciplines of two-year plans and quarterly targets, milestones and staged releases simply aren't going to work in this context, and letting go of them is hard for people who are used to that kind of predictability.

"Anyone coming to this from a corporate perspective is going to have to unlearn a number of acquired skills, unlearn reflexes and learn some new ones," he says. "You need a willingness and ability to reinvent your industry and yourself, to some extent. Not just using buzzwords and dressing a little differently, but genuinely in the way you run a business.

"It's a very different mindset. That mindset clashes with the established corporation all the time. People try to help, usually with the best of intentions, but frankly it's completely counterproductive."

Managers in traditional businesses are fundamentally risk-averse. They are trained to minimize risk and bred to fear failure. The manager who misses a target by, say, 5% has a problem. But anyone who expects to be able to forecast an entrepreneurial start-up's performance to the nearest 5% has a problem, too. Reality doesn't work like that. Unpredictability is built into the mix.

The entrepreneur – less concerned with predicting, more concerned with doing – knows the trade-offs between risk and reward, accepts the risk of failure and may even relish the vivid immediacy of living close to the edge.

Entrepreneurs may originally have been drawn towards working for themselves because of a powerful psychological desire for control, a wish to be able to set their own priorities and schedules, work with the people they choose to work with and enjoy gratifying feelings of freedom, self-direction and autonomy. That desire is a primitive, innate, deep-seated part of their personalities, and it's unlikely to change, except, perhaps, over the very long term.

As a result, entrepreneurs who have worked for themselves may be quite unable to imagine ever working for anyone else again – perhaps *with*, certainly not *for*. But having this urge to control your own life doesn't make you a control freak (despite what your friends say!). It's simply part of your identity, a part of who you are. And in terms of the individual's psychological needs, control may actually be more important than success.

Among serial entrepreneurs, there are few who haven't tasted disappointment, or even disaster. It's a tough way to live, and it brings inevitable casualties. But those who survive, who come through failure and bounce back for more, know that their experience is seldom wasted. "Was mich nicht umbringt, macht mich stärker," said Nietzsche – "What does not kill me makes me stronger." More than 130 years later, the world is very different, but the principle still holds good.

In fact, entrepreneurs often actively embrace failure. They don't enjoy it, of course, but they are good at making the most of it. Edison famously succeeded in inventing the carbon-filament electric light bulb by failing to invent it several hundred times first. Modern entrepreneurs are fond of the American saying "When life gives you lemons, make lemonade!" This principle is at the heart of the entrepreneur's expertise – the will to turn the unexpected into the profitable. While traditional business managers do all they can to avoid surprises, expert entrepreneurs learn to work with them and take advantage of them. In most contingency plans, surprises are seen as inherently negative – they usually represent the worst-case scenarios. But because entrepreneurs do not tie their ideas to theoretical or preconceived 'markets', every surprise is seen as holding the potential to be turned into a valuable opportunity.

The sort of self-confident, self-reliant individuals who set out on their own to launch high-tech businesses tend to think fast, decide fast and act fast. That's a luxury leaders of established corporations can't afford, because the negative implications of failure might be just too devastating. But individuals who self-select into entrepreneurship may be inspirational mavericks, fiercely logical scientists, geeky IT nerds or soft-spoken dreamers, male or female and from every kind of social background. Hollywood stereotypes are no use here, and a roomful of tech entrepreneurs tends to look much like any other assortment of bright, mostly young, people.

They do tend to have certain psychological traits in common, though. One is ambition, either personal ambition or an ambition to change society for the better. Often both. Another is an unusual ability to tolerate and live with ambiguity and uncertainty.

Entrepreneurs understand and accept that key decisions frequently have to be made on the basis of incomplete or inconclusive information, and that actions may have to be started with no clear view of the eventual consequences. This makes them more inclined than most to take a chance on experiments, pilot projects and test launches – and quicker than traditional managers to pull the plug and terminate an experiment if it is not working.

Outside the business, of course, it's widely believed that entrepreneurs have a perverse appetite for risk. On the whole, they don't. They just get good at managing it. And that doesn't mean they're not afraid. They may be terrified, but they learn to live with it. The entrepreneur's way is to try to cultivate a positive relationship with fear, using it as a guide and a stimulus for exploration and reflection.

It's a subject most people don't like to open up about, but Ida Tin, boss of the women's health app Clue, is typically frank. There's a taboo, she believes, and it's high time it was broken.

"Fear is the biggest brake on evolution," she says. "It's what makes people not learn as fast as they could and hide from problems they really could address. Fear makes people contract. It makes them do stupid things. Fear management should be part of leadership training.

"It's just so clear that you've got to get really good at managing your own fear, your team's fear, your investors' fear. We've just had an 'Ask me anything' session, with anonymous questions and people asking nasty questions they would never ask me face to face. They're addressing their fear, ventilating it, and that's fine. But if you don't have these moments of ventilation and release and taking care of this big, sticky elephant in the room, it's not healthy. And I don't think it's something that happens much in other organizations."

MAKING ENTREPRENEURIAL ACTIVITY A TEAM GAME

Despite some of the legends that have grown up around the gods of Silicon Valley, tech entrepreneurs are often good team players. Their goals and motivations are internally generated, so they are not good at taking orders, but they collaborate well in partnerships, as equals.

Today's innovators are no longer the lone madcap geniuses of yesteryear, with Einstein's hair and Frankenstein's obsession. They value working with the right people and organizations as much as – sometimes even more than – having the right idea.

Ideas can, and usually will, go through many changes and iterations before a product is refined and launched. Meticulous competitive analysis has fallen out of favour, at least until the later stages of development. Discovering whether the problem you're solving really is a problem is still important. But most entrepreneurs know that even that, in the early days, is probably less significant than lining up committed and enthusiastic partners that share your sense of purpose.

Purpose, mission, the Steve Jobs notion of making a dent in the universe – this is the kind of higher motivation that underpins the most successful collaborations between dedicated entrepreneurs and large, established organizations. But big businesses need to know their investments stand a good chance of being rewarded, and so do the entrepreneurs.

They may love doing what they do, but that doesn't mean they want to do it for love. Incentives are important, and the big businesses that have been best at getting what they need from collaborations with entrepreneurs have always made sure their junior partners get their share of the spoils.

Ping An, the tech-led Chinese giant that has done such a brilliant job of starting and integrating new platform-based businesses over the last few years, has helped make a lot of hardworking entrepreneur partners very rich indeed.

As Ping An's Chief Innovation Officer, Jonathan Larsen, told us in May 2020, a properly balanced incentive structure guarantees that people who achieve success in their entrepreneurial collaborations are strongly motivated to stay on and press ahead.

"In the case of Ping An Good Doctor, the main managers we needed came to us from Alibaba, and we combined them with key individuals from within Ping An, as we always do. All those people get very meaningful equity stakes as part of their compensation.

"They're often required to actually put their own money in as well, to invest in the shares at a very early stage. So as soon as the company does well, they can do extremely well, too. There are no catches, no limits to their upside – and we're talking about companies that could be worth a hundred times more over time."

Entrepreneurs who have spent their time in the trenches and won their battle honours do not necessarily want to start again from scratch, building a business from nothing at all and depending on the precarious scramble for VC money. They have plans and ventures they would like to develop and they envy the assets – things like a large customer base, supplier relationships, brands, patents and specialist expertise – that are available to large corporations. They know they could do great things, and make them happen fast, if only they could access the backing and resources to experiment and take the risks that could lead to significant breakthroughs.

What's needed is a format, a framework, within which entrepreneurial creativity can be brought together with big company assets in a productive, collaborative alliance that works for both sides. There has to be a modern, realistic way of combining the unconventional, improvisatory guerrilla mindset of the entrepreneur with the resources of the big battalions.

That framework, however, cannot be too prescriptive. Instead, its aim should simply be to create the right enabling environment.

As Larsen puts it: "A lot of people take a kind of strategic planning view of this thing, centred around the idea of some kind of theoretical, repeatable process. But I don't think there is a repeatable process for starting new businesses.

"There's a mindset, and there are some rules of thumb, of course. But each one is so different that forcing it into some generic process won't work. I don't know why you would do that, apart from letting someone somewhere feel pleased that they got to make a nice PowerPoint slide that says 'This is how it's done'."

One of our main motives for writing this book has been to cut through the nonsense that is so often talked about entrepreneurs and tech ventures, and to investigate how collaborations between large organizations and practical, experienced entrepreneurs can be set up and structured to give both sides what they want and need and create new digitally-enabled businesses. An important element in this – and one that is surprisingly often ignored – is the point of view of the entrepreneurs themselves.

WHAT'S REALLY UNIQUE ABOUT THE INNOVATION EXPERTS?

"When it comes to collaboration, everyone cherishes the value of mutual inspiration. But inspiration is the easiest thing." That's the view of Boris Marte, a remarkably successful corporate leader at Erste Group Bank. "The hardest thing is: Do we speak the same language? Can we benefit from each other? Can we interpret the knowledge? And are the structures ready?"

The whole field of new business models and tech entrepreneurship is littered with would-be experts. Politicians pontificate about building the industries of the future. Well-meaning academics theorize about a world that will never quite exist. But there are some people – a fairly small, but growing, group – who should be listened to with real care. They deserve our respect and attention, because they've already been there and done it.

So a key part of the research for our book has been a broad but targeted research programme, interviewing and collating the views of experienced practitioners whose credentials to talk about the entrepreneur's life and motivation are unassailably strong. Hearing these voices will be valuable to many leaders of traditional organizations, who may, so far, have had little direct personal contact with the sort of tech entrepreneurs they may want to work with in the near future.

To capture these points of view, we asked a cross-section of our tech entrepreneur and investor colleagues for their opinions. Our interviewees ranged from Markus Fuhrmann, co-founder of Delivery Hero, the 2011 start-up that is now valued at an astonishing $7 billion, to one of the old hands at this game, Rolf Schrömgens, who co-founded Trivago in 2005 and has seen his brainchild rise to a valuation of $2 billion, with a majority stake held by Expedia.

We've also talked in detail to Daniel Krauss, co-founder of the mighty FlixBus, which only started operations in 2013 and is already worth more than $2 billion, and Ida Tin, whose period tracking and women's health app, Clue, is already used by 12 million women in almost every country in the world. To shape the new normal, we will need to create new digital solutions, and there is a fine informal network of these tech entrepreneurs who are willing to share their experiences with us.

Like the top people in most businesses, technology entrepreneurs have to be leaders, with the ability to inspire people to follow them, even when the goal lies far over the horizon and the road ahead is strewn with problems and pitfalls. They have to be able to infect others with their passion and energy and the confidence that they know where they are going, even if that confidence is sometimes severely threatened. As Ida Tin explained, the pressure to grow and expand your leadership capabilities is sometimes unnerving.

"It's almost as if the trajectory of the company is completely correlated with your own growth as a leader," she told us. "It's actually scary, but it's a very close connection and you need to take it seriously. You have to develop the confidence to create your own reality, to create what you need and make the world walk around you more. For me, that's been a big learning process."

Entrepreneurial leaders need a lot of different attributes, some more obvious than others. As we interviewed and spent time with more and more of these high-achieving entrepreneurs, it became increasingly clear that they tend to have certain qualities in common. The balance between them varies from one individual to the next, but there are eight particular attributes that seem to be an essential part of the make-up of everyone who successfully launches a new business in this area.

1. **A SENSE OF MISSION** – Tech entrepreneurs feel an urgent need to make an impact and make a difference. Money comes into it, but it's almost always a secondary motivation. They want to change and improve the world – or at least their corner of it.

2. **BOLDNESS** – They don't just accept risk. They like to measure themselves against it. It's part of the thrill. They're not necessarily adrenalin junkies or extreme sport fans, but they do relish the speed and unpredictability of start-up life.

3. **DECISIVENESS** – They make things happen fast around them. Their ambition is to find a way to change the wheel while the car's still moving.

4. **ADAPTABILITY** – They learn by doing – by trying and failing and changing course without regrets. Successful tech entrepreneurs don't wait until they can be certain of success. They know where they need to get to and there may be a master plan, but if it's not working, they'll do something different.

5. **ATTENTION TO DETAIL** – They back up the big vision with a nitpicking, nuts-and-bolts knowledge of everything that's going on, how and when and why. It's their baby, and they want to know every freckle.

6. **RESILIENCE** – They are persistent, resilient and tenacious. Setbacks will occur and the entrepreneur may often be the only one with the energy and belief to keep going.

7. **CURIOSITY** – They learn quickly, sucking in ideas and information from all directions. Because they never know where the next good idea is coming from, they are surprisingly good listeners.

8. **FAITH IN TECHNOLOGY** – The entrepreneurs we spoke to love tech. They believe it can usually come up with a solution to any problem, as long as the problem is identified or reframed correctly.

Felix frequently likes to point out that, although many entrepreneurs undoubtedly enjoy risk, it really is a fallacy that they're all headlong and reckless in their attitudes towards it.

"It's quite the reverse, really," he says. "We do need to get over some of the mystical fairy tales that surround entrepreneurs. Reckless risk-taking is one of the myths.

"In fact, entrepreneurs – because they do operate, especially in the early days, in areas of high risk – are mostly incredibly risk-aware. They're constantly trying to assess probabilities, weigh up the situation and make sure they take only calculated risks."

Those risk calculations, though, are mostly very different from the sums corporate management disciplines encourage. That conventional calculus is based on extensive predictions of market size, penetration, share and margins, and it's intended to optimize the expected returns.

When entrepreneurs think about risk, they are focused much more on affordable losses – 'What am I prepared to lose?' – than on the expected returns, which are necessarily hugely hypothetical and close to pure guesswork in the context of a completely new venture. They concentrate on cultivating opportunities that will have low failure costs and that will generate more options for the future. Cheap failures can provide cheap, but immensely valuable, learning, which can be applied to the next iteration or the next wholly new idea.

THE INDIVIDUAL AND THE GROUP

No one could agree more than us with Harvard Business School's Clayton Christensen when he wrote: "Management is the most noble of professions, if it's practised well. No other occupation offers as many ways to help others learn and grow, take responsibility and be recognized for achievement and contribute to the success of a team."

The point is, though, that top managers play at the same level as top entrepreneurs, but in a different game with different rules. And we all need to be clear about those differences, if they are going to team up successfully.

Those attributes listed above make the entrepreneur's instincts quite different from the traditional managerial mindset, with its addiction to planning, its carefully calculated KPIs and its underlying assumption that tomorrow will always be very like today.

Of course, as we've been forcefully reminded by what's happened with Covid-19, tomorrow probably won't be like today. It can suddenly become unimaginably different. The best-laid plans can be torpedoed by circumstance, in ways that no scenario planning exercises can prepare you for.

But even without the trigger of cataclysmic external events, the business world and consumer markets can change with startling speed. It's no accident that the early histories of some of the most successful start-ups of the past two decades have included radical changes of direction. The polite word, of course, is 'pivot'. "We pivoted 180°, hurled ourselves into it and never looked back!" sounds wonderful, when it's seen with hindsight from a position of strength. At the time, with no guarantees of success, it can be unbelievably alarming and stressful. As Jonathan Larsen of Ping An reminded us recently, that's an experience many of the world's most well-known and successful entrepreneurs have been through.

"Look at the history of something like PayPal. It's a $170 billion company now, but when Elon Musk and all those famous people that were the PayPal mafia founded their company, its original intentions were totally different from what it does today. Completely and utterly different. And there were pivot points in its history when it could have gone in a totally different direction."

The tech entrepreneur's approach is more like that of a chess grandmaster than a corporate product manager. You've got to get the strategic thinking right, but the detailed planning and execution has to change according to circumstances. Garry Kasparov, possibly the greatest chess player of all time, used to claim he only ever looked three moves ahead. "You don't need more," he said. His victories stemmed from an extraordinary gift for seeing what was important in complex situations, a talent for pattern recognition and a deep intuition about the right way to develop his ideas, rather than an ability to scan through a universe of millions of possible move sequences. It was more than pure logic. And the most successful entrepreneurs have the same kinds of skill in their armoury. But they also have one important asset the lone chess player cannot draw on. They can collaborate and form partnerships, bringing in other resources and perspectives and creating teams to amplify their strengths and make up for their weaknesses.

Rolf Schrömgens of Trivago echoes Kasparov's thinking when he tells us how he and his colleagues built one of the world's most successful hotel comparison and booking companies. But it was always the collective intelligence of the team that drove the business forward.

"We were always focused on the problem we were trying to solve," he says. "But what we were doing to solve that problem changed over time. It was all about being agile and adaptive. I could only ever think through the next couple of steps, because we are always reacting to new information."

Trivago originally focused on maximizing the leads that were provided for booking agents. But that turned out to be the wrong metric. What really mattered, of course, was the number of actual hotel bookings. When the company shifted its target, concentrating fiercely on booking volume, it led to major changes in the way the platform was developed.

"We started relearning our business," he explains. "The new focus led us towards using AI technologies, so the system was self-learning. We had to put in a huge new infrastructure to enable the system to match people's preferences and provide a very high level of individualization."

For Delivery Hero's Markus Fuhrmann, the problem with many established corporations is a set of policies and attitudes that stack the odds against radical innovation. Large companies know they need to invest in the future, and they are happy to set aside budgets for conventional R&D work on new products and technologies. They are even comfortable with the idea of trial and error in the R&D area, because they know that is how new ideas come about. But they aren't usually so happy experimenting on a bigger scale, with new ventures and new business models.

"Corporate guys don't treat venture building as R&D," says Fuhrmann. "They aren't prepared to tolerate failure in the venture business like they would in an R&D project. They're always hedging their bets and looking for plausible deniability."

Even companies that know they need to change and progress to survive and fight back against disruptive competitors find it hard to give innovation the priority it demands. They don't like the short-term risks, and they won't put their most talented people in charge of innovation projects.

"The best people are already working in positions that are important to the company, so no one wants to move them across to something that's starting small and may have a very uncertain outcome," he says. "And why would the individuals concerned want to switch into a role that's high risk and takes a lot of energy and commitment – and that doesn't offer a comparable upside?

"So you get companies nodding in the direction of innovation but not really doing what's needed. The people who could be driving new initiatives are put on committees and innovation boards and they get to spend just a couple of hours a month on new initiatives."

At a time when political turmoil, growing protectionism, digital disruption and a global pandemic are combining to produce instability and uncertainty throughout the business environment, ignoring the tides of change and digging in to fight yesterday's battles is a recipe for trouble, or even disaster. Tapping into the energy, skills and mindset of proven tech entrepreneurs – if it is done right – can provide established corporations with a uniquely effective way to fight back against today's inertia and tomorrow's threats of disruption.

If you are thinking of working with entrepreneurs, there is an important distinction to be made that is illustrated in the following graphic. Ideally, you want to be making a completely fresh start, working with entrepreneurs who have no strings attached or prior commitments.

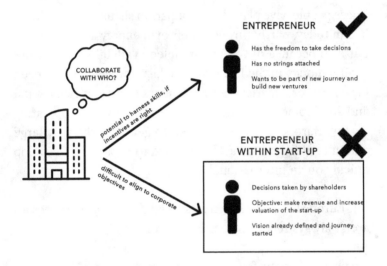

COLLABORATE WITH WHO?

potential to harness skills, if incentives are right

difficult to align to corporate objectives

ENTREPRENEUR ✔

Has the freedom to take decisions

Has no strings attached

Wants to be part of new journey and build new ventures

ENTREPRENEUR WITHIN START-UP ✘

Decisions taken by shareholders

Objective: make revenue and increase valuation of the start-up

Vision already defined and journey started

IT'S NOT JUST ABOUT SILICON VALLEY

When people think about the tech entrepreneurs of recent times, the picture is always dominated by the great American success stories. That's inevitable. That's where the media spotlight is trained – on the triumphs, the controversies, the world-scale philanthropy, the taxation arguments, the privacy issues and all the rest. Bill Gates and Steve Jobs, Mark Zuckerberg and Jeff Bezos, Elon Musk and Google's founders, Sergey Brin and Larry Page, have become household names.

Others who are only slightly less celebrated include Brian Chesky (Airbnb) and the co-founders of a string of worldwide brands – Jack Dorsey (Twitter), Travis Kalanick (Uber), Marc Benioff (Salesforce) and Drew Houston (Dropbox). Less well-known – and certainly less rich, but hugely influential – is Jimmy Wales, the driving force behind the internet's most important not-for-profit site, Wikipedia.

These people have played a major part in shaping the world we live in today, partly through their own energy and ingenuity, but also because of the unparalleled availability of venture capital money in the US. Until the last few years, it has been far easier for American entrepreneurs to attract risk capital and development funding than it has been for those operating in, say, Europe – and easier, too, to generate the very large amounts of financial backing needed to expand and develop quickly on an international scale.

But Europe has had its own hits, even if the biggest successes aren't always recognized as European.

Skype and Spotify, for example, are each as global as a brand can be. Yet Skype was originally created by a Swede, a Dane and a bunch of Estonian programmers, while Spotify's founder is Daniel Ek, a serial entrepreneur from Stockholm who had already made enough to retire for life before deciding to launch his innovative music streaming service.

Germany has produced Europe's largest online fashion retailer, Zalando (currently worth $11 billion), and mobile bank N26 (valued at $2.7 billion and part-funded by China's Tencent), as well as Trivago and Delivery Hero. Britain has spawned Rightmove (now part of the FTSE 100, with a market capitalization of $5 billion), Deliveroo (valued at $4 billion), ASOS (market cap: $3 billion) and Skyscanner ($2+ billion). Finnish entrepreneur Ilkka Paananen saw his *Clash of Clans* games company, Supercell, hit a valuation of more than $10 billion within six years of its 2010 launch, and London-based international money transfer service TransferWise (now worth $3.5 billion) was started by two expat Estonians. Even Poland has got in on the act. Its biggest e-commerce platform, Allegro, changed hands three years ago for $3.5 billion and is still growing fast.

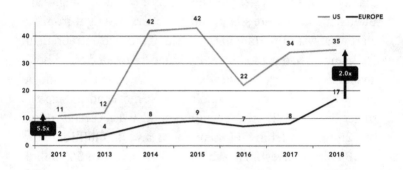

New unicorns in US and Europe:
EU starts to close the gap

ADAPTED FROM ATOMICO AND PITCHBOOK

We're not just talking about Europe here; it's only an example. In fact, if you look closely, there is plenty of evidence that virtually every country in the world can provide the ideas, skills and entrepreneurial mindset to create disruptive and fast-growing start-ups.

But the big surprise – certainly for the man in the street, who still tends to think of the world's tech entrepreneurs as being largely concentrated in the US – is the huge amount of dynamic entrepreneurial activity now taking place in China. The flagships for China's entrepreneurial revolution have been Alibaba and Tencent, the only two of the world's ten most valuable companies that are not American-based and American-owned.

Alibaba is the ultimate platform-based business. It began, in April 1999, as a B2B marketplace, founded in a modest apartment in Hangzhou by Jack Ma, a former English teacher.

Ma says he has never written a line of code or made a single sale. But his instincts were sound and he understood right from the start what was important in the world of the tech entrepreneur. He knew he had a good idea. He knew he needed to be bold, adaptable and aggressive in the way he implemented it. And he knew that the only way to exploit his first-mover advantage was to get big fast. Within a few months, he had secured funding of $25 million from Goldman Sachs and $20 million from SoftBank (an investment which grew to be worth $60 billion by the time Alibaba went public, in 2014). Since then, the Alibaba group has expanded into retailing, e-payments, cloud computing and artificial intelligence, eBay-like C2C services, media and entertainment. It is now valued at more than $500 billion, and Ma's personal fortune is worth $37 billion.

Even now, though, Ma's ambitions for Alibaba are those of a benign megalomaniac. By 2036, he says, he wants to have created 100 million jobs and have a customer base of 2 billion people.

Tencent, too, has grown over a period of 20 years, from an internet start-up based on instant messaging services to a giant conglomerate with interests in gaming, music, social media, e-commerce, payments and cloud, AI and machine learning technologies. Like Alibaba, it has also become a major investor in start-ups and developing businesses, backing hundreds of new ventures and providing funding worth tens of billions of dollars over the past five years.

With active support available from such deep-pocketed investors at home, as well as from overseas VCs newly conscious of the country's unique combination of technical resources and entrepreneurial potential, China is being seen as the land of opportunity. Silicon Valley may still be the hotbed of tech creativity, but China is rapidly becoming the world leader in business model innovation.

It has produced star performers like the ride-hailing service DiDi and the machine learning-powered content platform ByteDance (owner of TikTok), which are both valued at more than $70 billion, and at least 15 other start-ups, mostly unknown in the West, that are worth $5 billion or more.

Alongside thousands of ambitious ground-level start-ups, many of China's biggest companies have begun to adopt radical, risk-taking approaches to rethinking their businesses and launching new ventures. Ping An, for example, has branched out from being a sedate, conventional, Western-style life insurance company to exploit its platform and its huge customer base. It has created three hugely successful start-ups – peer-to-peer lender Lufax, Ping An Health Insurance and Ping An Good Doctor, which offers AI-driven health services – which are now valued at $39.4 billion, $9 billion and $11 billion, respectively.

THE RIGHT PEOPLE, IN THE RIGHT KIND OF PARTNERSHIP

The important point is that recent technological advances, new business models and the current availability of investment capital have opened up exciting opportunities for radically new ventures – not just in the vast economies of the US and China, but anywhere in the world.

The only piece of the jigsaw that's missing, in most cases, is the entrepreneurial talent to take a promising idea, develop and refine it and turn it into a scalable business that can grow fast and fulfil its potential.

One of the lessons of the past few years is that this does demand a particular kind of personality and mindset. You can't just take a clever, capable and experienced manager, used to dealing with the formal KPIs and cautious, risk-averse processes of traditional business models, and put him or her in charge of a fast-growing, mould-breaking start-up.

You might get lucky. There may be hidden flair that's waiting to be realized and given its head. But if you are looking for the drive, resilience, energy and ingenuity that will overcome obstacles and make things happen fast, your best bet is to collaborate with a hardened tech entrepreneur who has been through it all before – one who's felt the pain of failure and the thrill of success. There is just no substitute for experience in this area.

At the same time, it is important to match the individual to the task. Simply identifying someone with a track record of successful start-up activity is not enough. There are different types of tech entrepreneur, with different mindsets and skills. The person you need to come up with revolutionary, off-the-wall ideas may not be the right person to help you adapt and validate a new service or to grow a business fast enough to grab and hold your first-mover advantage. Who you choose to work with and how you set the businesses up and incentivize your chosen partners are critically important issues.

The fact is, though, there are too few entrepreneurs to go round.

Alongside all the business challenges and opportunities presented by our changing and digitizing world, there are any number of social and even global issues that are crying out for the kind of radical, technology-powered solutions that are most likely to come from aggressively entrepreneurial and inventive thinking.

The problems we need to tackle today tend to be multifaceted and highly complex. These days, it's not usually just about making or distributing things, like building a school or a bridge, printing a book or transporting washing machines or widgets from one place to another. The most pressing issues tend to be systemic or structural, with serious implications for communities, nations or even the future of the planet and its population.

From the biggest of them all – climate change, disease pandemics, hunger, poverty, biodiversity, war, education and human rights – to specific challenges like energy and water management, the health needs of ageing populations, terrorism, exposing corruption and building liveable cities and transport systems, the range is endless. Being an entrepreneur is not always about trying to conjure up a billion-dollar unicorn. While there are obviously plenty of entrepreneurs who are mainly concerned with achieving wealth and success, there are many more whose energy, idealism and sense of social purpose could potentially create new solutions to these big global problems. Ambition comes in many forms, and there will be many opportunities for these people to combine their own personal goals with the more altruistic drive to make the world a better place.

The examples are already there for all to see.

Elon Musk's Tesla is on track to sell half a million electric cars a year, and it also supplies power trains for other car manufacturers, such as Daimler and Toyota. Musk has not been shy about his business ambitions, in everything from solar panels to space exploration, but he has stated many times that helping to reduce global warming is a personal obsession. His promotion of electric vehicles has been a significant factor in a trend that is clearly having a positive global impact.

When Jack Ma of Alibaba talks about creating 100 million new jobs by 2036, he's not just thinking about growing his company's profits. Even if he falls far short of this figure, he will have provided incomes and opportunities for millions of families.

The concept of financial trickle-down – the idea that low taxes on personal wealth allow the extremely rich to invest and spend money in ways that eventually benefit the less well-off – has always been controversial and now has many vociferous opponents among both left-wing and right-wing economists. But the idea of technological and even social trickle-down – the notion that tech innovation, even if it starts off by benefiting the few, frequently has the potential to bring a broad range of benefits to everyone – is entirely plausible.

Innovative platform-based businesses have already shown that they can do this. Amazon and eBay have made it possible for consumers in remote locations to find the lowest prices and order what they want without travelling to specialist retailers to make their purchases. Uber, Lyft and DiDi have enabled people who could not afford conventional taxis to get from A to B, or even to get rid of their cars. FlixBus allows students and pensioners to make long-distance journeys they could never previously afford, and Airbnb makes staying in a strange city possible for travellers on any kind of budget.

So the entrepreneur's significance and impact in society is not solely concerned with the ability to create profitable new businesses. All of these international success stories can be seen as having brought real improvements to millions of lives, but none of them has been set up as a charitable nonprofit organization. In each case, the good they have done has come as a direct result of their success in spotting a gap and building a business based on satisfying a previously unrecognized need. In today's changing global circumstances, with the world battered by Covid-19 and threatened by the even bigger disaster of climate change, there is a real need for the same kind of dynamism to be applied to issues that go far beyond the creation of private wealth and touch on the very survival of our civilization.

Many large organizations have tried to kick-start their digital transformation via acquisitions, buying up promising start-ups in the hope of capturing some of the digital know-how and entrepreneurial energy they find so hard to develop. But an existing start-up will already have its own shareholders and its own agenda, which is highly unlikely to align exactly with your own.

The chances of successfully launching new and strategically relevant ventures that will develop into valuable businesses, benefit your core organization and even create the possibility of making the world a better place are very much higher if you can work, right from the start, with the right highly-qualified and strongly-motivated individual entrepreneurs, within a practical, realistic framework that is designed to foster collaborative co-creation.

The previous two sections and this one should have shown you that we all have the opportunity now to create meaningful change. We've seen how data-driven technologies can help advance value-based healthcare and reduce carbon emissions. And we have discovered, for example, how digital platforms can help us make healthier choices for ourselves and our planet.

In the next chapter, we will look at a structured, tried and tested approach that can enable established organizations and tech entrepreneurs to work together to devise, launch and scale the kind of high-growth digital initiatives that can transform the future of your organization and, potentially, have an impact on the world around you. This is not a mission for the private sector alone. As you will see in our case study from Estonia, there is now a key role for hybrid leaders, like Taavi Kotka, who can create new connections between the public sector and the world of business.

KEY CONCEPTS

1. EVERYDAY ENTREPRENEURS
There's a potential entrepreneur inside almost all of us. Look around and you'll see grassroots innovators everywhere, at local and regional levels, solving everyday problems in meaningful and inventive ways.

2. A DIFFERENT VIEW OF UNCERTAINTY
The hugely successful, headline-grabbing entrepreneurs we know by name all share some particular traits. They aren't necessarily the dashing, risk-hungry adventurers of popular legend, but their mindset – and particularly how they deal with uncertainty and fear – is often very different from those of corporate leaders.

3. THE SECRET IS LIFELONG UNLEARNING

Successful entrepreneurial collaborations usually depend more on people's adaptability and readiness to unlearn old ways than on any particular ability to feed off past experience or learn new skills.

OUR KEY RECOMMENDATIONS FOR YOU:

- All of us have something of the entrepreneur in our make-up – and innovation doesn't always come from the designated innovators. We need to empower people to think big, think differently and come up with ideas to change their work, their lives and the world.

- It makes sense to encourage individuals with entrepreneurial talent inside your core organization. But to exploit your assets in new digital businesses in new markets you'll need a particular type of structure. You'll need a dedicated operating model that can accommodate experienced entrepreneurs, while maintaining close connections with supportive C-level sponsors.

- Working closely with experienced entrepreneurs – and we firmly believe you should want to do that – means understanding that you will probably be dealing with a very different mindset. Success will depend on developing the ability to appreciate each other's skills and ways of thinking.

- The trick is to find the right problem to solve. Always be in love with the problem, not a particular solution. Be ruthless about killing your darlings and letting go of your initial ideas.

- Unlearning the skills and disciplines that have taken you to the top – or at least recognizing when they might need to be set aside – is an important element in taking on new challenges. Working with entrepreneurs to create new ideas and launch new businesses can be an invigorating and rewarding experience, but it may sometimes require the kind of leap of faith that corporate cultures don't usually encourage.

COLLECTIVE GENIUS

Linda Hill is not your average academic. She is the sort who likes to get her hands dirty. She has served on the boards of three Fortune 500 corporations, worked with Bertelsmann, Volkswagen, Accenture, Salesforce.com and dozens of other big companies and advised NASA on how to reignite its innovative drive. She has co-written a string of bestselling business books, including *Collective Genius: The Art and Practice of Leading Innovation, Being the Boss* and *Becoming a Manager.* Now she's getting a feel for the tech entrepreneur's perspective, as a board member of an ambitious biotech start-up.

"I'm having fun, being with a start-up," she says. "It's my first time, seeing how investors operate and all the rest of it. I've been brought in to help them think about scaling and the associated leadership and cultural challenges."

In her day job, Hill is the Wallace Brett Donham Professor of Business Administration at Harvard Business School and chair of the HBS Leadership Initiative. She has a lot of irons in the fire, but one project she's engaged in with consulting firm Egon Zehnder, among others, leverages her work with veteran IT strategist Jim Cash to help boards make better decisions about digital technology and digital transformation.

This project has already highlighted some largely unrecognized issues.

"Too often, boards try to find their one digital expert," she says. "Of course, one person can't be the expert about all that is digital.

"There's one study that claims that unless you have at least three people on the board who have significant digital experience, the board doesn't really get any better at making decisions about digital technology. In fact, the whole board must have some foundation or shared literacy about digital matters if they are to be in a position to help management navigate the digital space."

The problem may be partly a generational issue. The next generation of directors should be more digitally savvy, since they have grown up in a pervasively digital world. For instance, they know at first hand the power of social media. But, of course, many boards are often reluctant to bring in younger – by definition, less experienced – board members.

In Hill's research and consulting work, she has seen many companies that have made major investments in digital tools, or building out platforms, but never achieved their ambitions to increase innovation and provide differentiated customer experiences.

"Incumbent companies find that they cannot get the full benefit of their investments unless they can get people to work differently," she says. "And that means changing culture and organizational capabilities.

"You can give people AI or Big Data analytics, but do they know how to run quick and dirty experiments or collaborate in cross-functional teams to learn from those experiments? They rarely get better at finding solutions to problems their customers really care about."

She sees today's established organizations as often too slow to understand the threats from competitors other than the known rivals within their own industries.

These disruptive outsiders may have a wider field of vision, focusing on what *could* be done in an industry, rather than what is already recognized as what *should* be done. When these new competitors do the *could*, that becomes your *should* – and the nature of the game is changed for ever.

Technology often plays a big part in all this, but it needs to be there in the service of developing a business model that will allow a company to deliver what customers value.

"One of the things you know, if you're an entrepreneur, is that you don't lead with the technology," says Hill. "What you lead with is whatever the customer is going to need or want. The digital part is just the tool that helps you do that."

Ideas come from people, not technologies. But Hill's research focus on leadership and innovation has convinced her that it's almost invariably the cross-fertilization of diverse ideas within a team that creates new paradigms and radically new offerings.

"Innovation is not about solo genius," she says. "It's about collective genius."

Unleashing that genius is about putting the right people together and placing them in an environment that encourages them to share and leverage their talents and passions. That means breaking down the walls between those who are supposed to innovate and those who are supposed to execute. It's something incumbent corporations find hard to do, though it's second nature to tech entrepreneurs.

"When you're in an entrepreneurial setting, there's not that division," she says. "Everybody is both innovating and executing."

Shifting to this new kind of entrepreneurial working environment requires a new mindset and a different and more subtle approach to leadership. It can no longer be about positioning yourself as a leader and saying, 'Hey, people, follow me.' The responsibility is shared across the team.

"To co-create the future we want to build together, everybody has the responsibility to be a value creator and a game changer," says Hill.

"We all know how hard innovation is. When companies bring in methodologies like lean start-up or design thinking, what they're doing is trying to get people to use muscles they haven't used before and to think in different ways.

"All these ideas are about trying to help people learn to be more like entrepreneurs in the way they work."

'ABOVE ALL, THE CDO SHOULD REPORT DIRECTLY TO THE CEO'

Rahmyn Kress combines many lives in one person. He's the founder of the HumanCapitalNetwork, a serial entrepreneur, investor and technologist. He is a sought-after pioneer of change with the entrepreneurial vision, business acumen and social commitment needed to thrive in today's marketplace. When we interviewed him for this book, Rahmyn was Chief Digital Officer (CDO) for Henkel, a global leader in laundry and homecare, beauty products and adhesives. The company had been operating for 143 years and its brands – familiar names like Persil detergent, Schwarzkopf hair products and Loctite glues – were generating worldwide sales of more than $22 billion a year.

But history and tradition don't guarantee success, or even survival, in the consumer packaged goods sector, any more than they do in more obviously vulnerable industries like retailing or media. The disrupters are coming, and Kress's job was driving the changes that would make Henkel ready to take its place in a digital world.

That's not something the consumer packaged goods industry has generally been good at doing. A lot of big, long-established companies in these areas have been slow out of the blocks. And those that have set out on the road to digital transformation have not always shown much of a talent for it.

"I don't think I've seen one single consumer packaged goods company that is actually doing it right," says Kress. "A lot of them are coming very late to the party."

He was with Henkel for just over two years, in a key position that he ended up in more or less by accident. He'd been called in to give his advice on what the company should look for in its quest to hire a CDO, advice he handed out with the robust candour of an informed outsider.

"I was very blunt. I asked them: 'Do you know why you want a CDO? Do you know what you want him to achieve? Is this just because everyone else has one?'

"I told them they should have a clear idea of the remit – what this person should do and not do – and, above all, that the CDO should report directly to the CEO, nobody else. And then they asked me to take the job."

Kress believes no CDO should ever stay in the role for more than three years. There has to be a sense of urgency if you are going to drive a radical change agenda. In his two years at Henkel, he hurried to put in place the first stage of the company's digital trans-formation. He identified and built the basics of the digital technology stack, and brought in new eCRM and performance marketing initiatives, before handing these tools back into the care of the core organization's traditional IT and marketing teams.

But his biggest initiative was the launch of Henkel X, a revolutionary innovation platform that has attracted attention around the world.

Henkel X was launched in February 2018. The aim was
to establish a rich, collaborative network that would
bring together Henkel's business partners, big companies, successful entrepreneurs, venture capital firms
and start-ups. There would be plenty of room for ideas
and discussion, but Kress wanted it to be a vehicle
for action as well. There have been seven Henkel X
show-and-tell events already and the results have been
extremely encouraging.

"We've had 18 proof-of-concept projects emerging
from this activity, and it's led to six long-term partnership agreements so far," he says.

Kress has his own ideas about how large corporations
should approach the challenges of working productively with entrepreneurs and start-ups, and he is not a
fan of 'innovation tourism' and the faddish attempts to
stimulate creativity he sees around him.

"I don't believe in accelerators or incubators," he snorts.
"I've seen too many that fail and too few that succeed."

He believes that big companies engaging with start-ups
often go about it the wrong way, killing the goose that
could, potentially, lay the golden egg. They are too
focused on control, too keen to throw money at the
problems that come up and too cynical about using and
discarding their junior partners.

"You've got to do it the right way," he says. "That means
treating them with respect. They're little companies.
Don't exploit them, bring them in as wacky consultants
and then spit them out. Don't over-invest and kill them

that way. And you must leave them the freedom to do what you've brought them in to do in the first place. Corporations are generally very bad at this.

"You need to find a framework, an operating model, that allows room for these collaborative activities to flourish. I don't believe for a second that you can do it on your own."

Kress has developed his broad, cross-industry perspective over the course of a career that's seen him create high-tech companies, work in the music business, for Universal Music Group, and lead Accenture's ecosystem and ventures strategy.

"We do need to be leading a fightback," he says. "But it's not a fightback against disruption. Those changes are inevitable. It's a fightback against our own fear and inertia. The impact that digital technology and platforms have had in other industries is telling companies like ours that they must come up with new models and services if they want to remain relevant.

"But if you do it, and you do it successfully, a large proportion of your business will eventually drive into digital."

'MOVE FAST AND BREAK THINGS DOESN'T WORK HERE'

Think of an iconic duo that's shaped an industry. Financial services? Warren Buffett and Charlie Munger. Internet? Sergey Brin and Larry Page. Medical artificial intelligence? It might well be Claire and Daniel of Ada Health. That's Dr Claire Novorol and Daniel Nathrath. Together with their third co-founder, Professor Martin Hirsch, they've created the world's fastest-growing medical app, empowering people across the world to make more informed decisions about their health. Over 10 million downloads and 18 million health assessments later, telehealth seems to be in safe hands.

To overcome healthcare worker shortages, Ada deploys technology to leverage medical knowledge and bring it directly to end-users. It works pretty much as if you had 24/7 access to your trusted family doctor, and you could wake him or her up in the middle of the night and say, "I'd like to have a WhatsApp chat with you."

You can send a message explaining what's bothering you and Ada will ask you questions, very much like a good doctor would when taking a patient history. At the end of that, the app gives you an idea of what you might be suffering from and recommendations on what to do next. The ambition is not to replace the doctor, but to support the user to make a more informed decision on next steps, and then be able to share the outcome of this pre-assessment with the health professional. That way, the doctor or nurse who meets a patient face-to-face is already pre-briefed.

The founders are famous in the healthcare field for their deep dedication to creating meaningful change.

"There have been, and still are, a number of mis-aligned incentives in healthcare," Novorol says. "Sometimes the way things happen isn't necessarily in the best interests of the patient. New digital health companies have an opportunity and a responsibility to push for things to move towards what's right for the patient and to make healthcare more accessible, affordable and sustainable."

The mission is laudable, but it is a challenge to get such transformative technology into a complex and established system.

For Nathrath, this came as a surprise. "Back then, when we started, doctors weren't necessarily the earliest adopters of new technologies. I knew about some of the conservative forces in the healthcare system. But I'd already worked in tech for 15 years and I was used to building lean start-ups – you know, build an MVP (minimum viable product), iterate, get going and generate some revenue. So I was naïve about how quickly you could move things in healthcare. 'Move fast and break things' doesn't really work here."

Novorol, being an insider in the healthcare system, was less surprised. When she started working on Ada they were not looking to build an MVP. Instead, they were "really very focused on building an absolute best-in-class, best-in-the-world probabilistic medical reasoning technology," she says. "And that took years."

Still, looking back, she would have taken some lessons from the 'lean start-up' playbook. "What I wish we had started doing sooner and done more of is fail-fast rapid experimentation early on to road test an idea. And not just product innovations, but business model innovation, too. We could have learned what wasn't going to work, what was more likely to work, pivoted and really de-risked before putting a lot of resources in."

Ada started as a decision-support tool to assist specialists by automating parts of their history-taking and helping them find the right diagnosis faster. Then, the team focused on expanding the knowledge base to cover general practice, because they found hints that the majority of delayed or missed diagnoses happened much earlier in the patient's journey, at the general practitioner stage. So they moved upstream, from specialists to GPs. But it turned out that doctors were not keen on using Ada in their daily working life – perhaps through fear that such apps would eventually make them redundant, or because of problems connecting Ada into the legacy systems needed for billing.

At the same time, Novorol and Nathrath saw increasing interest coming from the patients themselves and decided to move one step further upstream. That meant translating their already very extensive medical knowledge base into patient-friendly language.

Nathrath likes to refer to a key lesson they learned from the late, great Clayton Christensen of Harvard Business School. "The risk is that if you are a new entrant in an industry and you work with the incumbents,

they usually capture most of the value and they win,"
he says. "If you have not just a technological innovation, but also a disruptive business model, then you
have an opportunity to make it really big.

"And that is a big challenge in healthcare. Because, on
the one hand, you have pressure from investors – even
though we are very lucky with ours. You need to generate revenue, and the best way to generate revenue
is to work with the incumbents. On the other hand, if
you really want to land a moonshot, then you have to
try and change the way the incumbents play the game,
rather than play their game. That's a challenge I think a
lot of young digital health companies have been facing
and will continue to face."

Even with such a strong founding team that brings
together all the necessary skills and mindsets, establishing something like Ada would not have been
possible without the ongoing financial support of a
couple of wealthy German families. "They have been
extremely patient with us for the first seven years,"
Nathrath says. "They kept finding new relatives to help
us, because they believed in the mission of the company – and, to some extent, believed in us. It's a big
responsibility for us."

ESTONISHING!

What's better – being a big fish in a little pond or a small fish in a big pond? Taavi Kotka has shown us it doesn't matter that much, as long as it's a cutting-edge pond. He was the first-ever CIO for the Government of Estonia and the pioneer behind e-Estonia, helping earn Estonians a reputation as the world's most advanced digital nation. Co-founder of the world's first e-residency programme, Kotka has made a name for himself in entrepreneurship and public speaking, too. Sometimes you can tell the pond by the fish that swim in it.

It was a unique role, as national CIO, and Kotka introduced some unique and revolutionary ideas that marked Estonia as the most digital country in Europe. They included e-residency, data embassies and the 'country-as-a-service' concept.

E-residency, for example, allows people in other countries to start and run businesses in Estonia.

"It enables us to increase the number of people who are connected with Estonia economically, without forcing those people to come and live here," Kotka explains. "They can live wherever they want to live and still be part of our economy. A German citizen, for example, could set up her company in Estonia rather than Germany and still pay her income tax at home. But Germany doesn't get her company tax any more.

"Only Estonia and a couple of other small countries are doing this. But imagine if China did it. What if China

said to the Generation Y and Generation Z entrepreneurs: 'Why start your business in Germany? Come and
create a virtual company in China. We can offer you a
huge market, global access, low costs, no hassles'? We
could lose whole generations of tech entrepreneurs."

Estonia went digital because it had to. It felt the pain
and realized the only way to run the country and serve
a thinly-distributed population was to get everyone
doing as much as possible online.

"Our country is tiny, in terms of population, with just
1.3 million people," he says. "But in terms of land area,
we are big – bigger than Switzerland, or Belgium, or
the Netherlands. If you spread one million or so people
over a land this size, you soon discover that you can't
afford to have a bank branch in every small town or
government offices everywhere."

And so the private sector started pushing people
towards self-service, towards using the internet. That
meant that the digital identity issue became very
important – you had to be able to be sure about who
was behind the computer.

"The government worked with the banks and telcos
to solve the digital ID problem, and then followed the
same path itself, in order to become more efficient.
Going paperless in many areas meant we could concentrate on more meaningful tasks."

Given the close collaboration between the government
and the private sector, it's no coincidence that Estonia
is one of the fastest-growing EU economies and

has the highest income per head of any of the ex-Soviet republics – by a clear 30%. That tiny population has made a big splash in the digital world.

The same tech skills that have created Estonia's young generation of can-do entrepreneurs have made their mark on civil society as well. Filing a tax return is a three-click job, and connectedness saves lives when paramedics can get instant access to an accident victim's full medical records. People have quickly become used to a digitally streamlined, largely hassle-free life.

"There are no queues in Estonia," says Kotka. "I went through New York's JFK Airport with my children. When they saw all the ropes marking out the lines for the immigration desk, they asked me: 'What is that?' They'd never seen a queue in their lives."

SECTION 5

CORPORATE VENTURE BUILDING
HELPS YOU FIGHT BACK AGAINST
OUR BIGGEST CHALLENGES,
USING YOUR EXISTING ASSETS

INNOVATING FOR IMPACT

Imagine a simple, popular consumer app that helped to save the world from climate change by making it easy for millions of people to set and keep to their own personal 'planet impact budgets', tracking them in real time – Am I walking enough? Can I take another flight? Am I using the hot tub too much?

Imagine a fully regulated and approved healthcare app, a 'Doctor in your Pocket' that would give you instant access to online health monitoring – pulse, blood pressure, glucose levels, perhaps even scanning your face and eyes for warning signs of ill health.

Imagine a new asset class that brings together our best and most inventive brains and the power and resources of our big companies, government agencies, universities and communities to create amazing new solutions to our world's most urgent problems.

Don't worry too much about the term asset class. It sounds technical, but it just refers to a structured way of investing capital, time and other resources, like data and intellectual property, in order to create new value.

The innovation industry has been making great profits so far, not always for the benefit of its corporate clients. But if you want to become – or remain – a leader in the new normal, it's important not to waste your time and resources chasing rainbows and hunting unicorns.

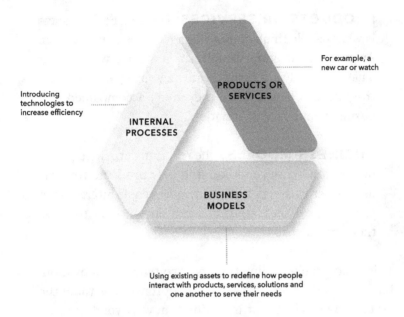

For example, a
new car or watch

**PRODUCTS OR
SERVICES**

Introducing
technologies to
increase efficiency

**INTERNAL
PROCESSES**

**BUSINESS
MODELS**

Using existing assets to redefine how people
interact with products, services, solutions and
one another to serve their needs

Product, process and business model innovation

In considering the different types of innovation approach, we are generally looking at three elements – processes, products and business models, as shown in the graphic above.

1. **INTERNAL PROCESSES:** Your business processes can, of course, be optimized. This can be done, for example, by installing technologies to increase the efficiency of what you already do. Machine learning, AI and advanced robotics may play a huge role in this in the years ahead. This optimization is vitally important in order to stay competitive, but it typically leads to nothing more than incremental innovation. You should probably have been doing this anyway.

2. **PRODUCTS OR SERVICES**: Devising new products is what people think of first when it comes to innovation. An auto manufacturer launches a new car, a watchmaker a new watch. These items create new value, but are rarely truly transformative when they aren't accompanied by a business model transformation.

3. **BUSINESS MODELS**: The real transformative power lies in moving beyond building new products towards using existing assets to redefine how people interact with products, services, solutions and one another to serve their specific needs.

This is not to undermine the first two types of innovation. Business model transformation cannot function without the other two elements. But if we don't move beyond that, we won't alter the way we operate. You won't be able to tackle the large health and climate issues. And it won't make you a shaper of the new normal.

In the face of the biggest global threats, we need to use all our assets differently, from new technologies and real-time data, to supplier relationships, distribution channels and everything else we have at our disposal. Uniting inventive forces through aligned incentives is the key to taking control of our destiny, at every level, and finding innovative answers to today's troubling, sometimes overwhelming, challenges.

In relation to issues like climate, disease pandemics, food security and waste management, we need to make sure our best ideas, technologies and expertise can be brought to bear at the precise points where they can make the most difference.

We have access to most of the technologies we might need. The problem is that it's not easy to leverage the existing assets of corporations to fuel the launch and growth of new digital businesses in a productive, purposeful manner. People's cultures, backgrounds and experience differ, and these differences get in the way of our ability to fulfil our potential in business, government and society.

The measure of humanity's tragedy will be the distance between what we could have done with our assets (technologies, connections, data and so on) and what we will actually achieve to ward off global disaster. Who wants to be the one to tell our children and grandchildren that we had all the technologies we needed to control the climate and keep us healthy, but were so busy putting Post-its on walls and engaging in politicized board meetings that we didn't get round to using our inventive muscle to solve the problems that really mattered?

What we are going to be talking about in the next few pages is corporate venture building – a new asset class that helps you invest in the future of your company, while potentially contributing to the resolution of society's challenges. At its core, corporate venture building (often just known by its initials, CVB) is an asset class – alongside M&A (as an approach to consolidating assets) and venture capital – that is designed to be better suited to tackle the problems that occur in complex, science-based, regulated and otherwise hard-to-handle markets.

To put everything into context, we will explore the strengths and weaknesses of the other commonly used asset classes and approaches to corporate innovation before moving on to talk about CVB.

	INVESTMENT TYPES			INNOVATION TOOLS	
	CVB	M&A	CVC	LABS/HUBS	ACCELERATOR
CONTROL	●	●	◕	●	◕
STRATEGIC ALIGNMENT	●	●	◕	○	◔
IMPACT ON CORE P&L	●	●	◔	◔	◔
POTENTIAL IMPACT ON CLIMATE & HEALTH	●	●	●	○	○
REGULATED INDUSTRIES	●	◑	○	◕	◕

Overview of growth initiatives

Just one more thing before we dive in. The following illustration is a reminder of the various stages of a venture, from inception to scale-up. It will help if you bear these in mind as we look at the range of tools available to help us create new digital businesses.

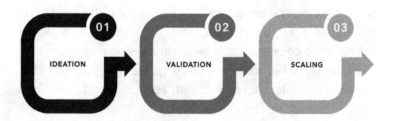

Innovation comes in stages, and the buzzwords for each stage have entered the mainstream business vocabulary. In the beginning, there is the lightbulb moment. Innovation typically starts with ideation, using basic brainstorming sessions and creative methodologies like Google sprints or design thinking, including the production and initial testing of rough and ready low-fidelity prototypes. Next comes the validation stage, with elements like scenario planning and the creation of minimum viable products. When this generates enough confidence to start ramping up sales, the scaling stage is reached, usually accompanied by a range of market simulations and forecasts. The problem here is that these activities often happen in a chaotic way, in the wrong order or as unsystematic efforts within an organization. What's missing is a concerted, focused and systematic approach. We'll get to that.

Venture capital successes may make for striking headlines, but VC models are not generally good at sparking fundamental change in complex areas like climate and health. The shortfalls have become pretty apparent, leading to well-intentioned initiatives like Google X (now known just as X) and the Bill Gates-led Breakthrough Energy Ventures, which is specifically focused on 'fighting climate change by investing in clean energy innovation'. Their efforts are laudable, but the truth is that examples like this are few and far between.

In fact, venture capital is typically biased towards business models that have the potential for rapid exponential growth. And even then, the results don't often live up to the hype. As Ping An's Jonathan Larsen points out: "The returns on venture capital for the last 25 years are dominated by a very small number of venture firms. If you look inside their port-folios, they are in turn dominated by a very small number of companies – Google, Facebook, Netflix, PayPal, and so on, and Airbnb and Uber, of course. But when you take those companies out, average returns for the whole venture capital world are something like 2.6%."

What's more, though they like to play for high stakes, VCs are often surprisingly risk-averse. They like to fund businesses with the potential to generate a revenue stream quickly and without too much in the way of external dependencies. Highly regulated markets, science-based businesses and industries marked by entrenched cultures and guarded by many stakeholders with vested interests to protect are not their preferred targets. VCs tend to gravitate to areas where the usual economic rules apply and 'unnecessary' risks are fairly well controlled, or at least calculable. But, as we explained in Section 3, the industries that are tackling our biggest health and climate challenges typically suffer from all of these drawbacks. Remember our graphic on the rate-limiting steps?

What we need now is something that captures some of the dynamism of the VC approach, while accommodating a wider range of industries and offering the chance to address a broader range of goals. In the words of Gerard Grech of Tech Nation, a growth platform for tech companies and leaders, " The venture capital model is a high-risk, high-stakes approach, which is at one extreme of the business spectrum. At the other end of the spectrum, you have academic institutions, NGOs and foundations, with little competition, delivering limited value. What's the best model for a new type of growth? Are we now grown-up enough to know that it is nuanced? It's not one or the other. Can we make those two cross-breed and generate extreme value? That is why this is one of the most exciting times right now – because of the change and opportunity."

Large, long-established organizations that are keen to respond to that change and grasp that opportunity may decide to try to mimic the VC approach in-house and back a portfolio of new start-up businesses of their own. This kind of corporate venture capital (CVC) activity may be prompted by several different motives. The intention may be to create fresh sources of revenue for the future, to help defend their existing territory or to benefit from some useful knowledge or cultural spillover from their portfolio companies. When reality strikes, they realize how little transfer really happens, in either direction. Attracting pitches from entrepreneurs who are starting up on their own can provide an innovation radar of sorts, and it can make sense to seek financial returns through early investment in high-growth companies. But the journey is long, usually seven years or more, and generating a good rate of return on your investment (even with expert knowledge and access) is difficult against strong competition from commercial VCs. Whatever high hopes the corporation sets out with, most investments will inevitably fail.

For Peter Borchers, founder of hub:raum, Telekom's global seed investor and sandbox, and former CEO of Allianz X, the Allianz group's $500m fund, the strategic element is likely to be the most significant. He sees corporate venture capital's main value as being its ability to provide strategic hedging against the threat of future disruption, rather than any capacity to foster short- or mid-term business opportunities.

But it is difficult to find a structure and format that will make the CVC approach work, especially because of the inevitable disparity in size and power between the mighty corporation and the new business.

"If you decide to do something that can provide a substitute for your core business," Alexander Wennergren Helm of Doktor24 tells us, "you really have to do it as a separate entity. It's very hard to do it internally. Big corporations are structured to keep the core functioning. You're going to have internal conflict, and you cannot get the necessary cooperation working."

The realities of the situation dictate that the requirements, assumptions and financial disciplines of the core business will always tend to overshadow the needs of the junior partner. With the best will in the world, it is almost impossible for a large corporation to relax its grip and give the growing business the patient, unconditional support and freedom to make mistakes that will allow the entrepreneurial newcomer to do what it has to do.

Alex Manson, who sits on the corporate side, launching new businesses as the head of Standard Chartered's SC Ventures, recognizes the problems such lopsided CVC collaborations often face. "Not everyone is culturally suited to the type of partnership we need now," he says. "It takes an element of empathy and an element of humility."

Given the obvious difficulties of making corporate venture capital projects work, many business leaders choose to resort to M&A, hoping that all their problems can be solved by moving further downstream in the venture creation process. This is usually misguided. If there's already a bias in the venture capital system against start-ups that tackle complex and entrenched markets, how likely is it that that's going to change downstream?

The big issue with M&A, in our view, is that business leaders think acquisitions are less risky because the start-ups they buy have already proved themselves in the market. They hugely underestimate the risks that come with integrating the new company, as we'll be discussing later, when we talk about Phase 3 of the corporate venture building approach.

To sum up the problem: if you want to tackle the big challenges of society, who do you want to buy that is going to help you achieve that?

There's also another, very straightforward, consideration. Acquiring a digital business doesn't turn you into a digital master. If you can gain front-line, first-hand experience within your own organization, it helps ensure that you will be able to connect with external start-ups and understand their strengths and weaknesses.

That points back to the other option, of course, of building your own digital business, rather than buying one. Markus Homann, who leads a corporate venture for Italy's Generali, one of Europe's largest international insurers, is clear about why his group prefers building to buying.

"If you buy a start-up, the chances are that it will already have a strong culture," he says. "Either you leave it as it is, or you kill it – and both options are problematic. If you are going to leave it as it is, why buy it in the first place and not buy software-as-a-service? If you kill it, it's obvious that this is not good.

"A big factor in the thinking about how we get innovation and make healthcare better is that starting our own company allows us to create a strong company culture and have a vehicle, based on that culture, that can do things that would be impossible in a command-and-control environment."

The start-ups that are available to be acquired at any given time are likely to have several things in common. By the time they appear on the corporate's radar, they have probably already gathered enough momentum and confidence to guarantee the price will be too high. The entrepreneurs will have created their own culture and set their own goals and they'll be convinced they've located their core customer base. Start-up founders typically aim for growth first, in order to attract the next funding round. They are heading off on their own track, dreaming dreams of wealth and glory and making a difference. So what will buying these external start-ups do to help your P&L or provide you with future strategy options?

Of course, you do see some independent start-ups that grow under their own steam and later pivot towards bigger value propositions and fight for regulatory approval. But they will all have to follow the same market logic, just to survive. If you can raise a VC funding round, you may get the money, but you'll always be under pressure, because you are constantly racing against the clock. That means you need to find lots of customers as fast as possible to prove you have solved an important problem and made something people actually want. In that situation, getting bogged down in regulatory delays is the last thing you need.

For people growing successful stand-alone healthcare start-ups, like Ada Health and Clue, securing the necessary approvals from regulators like America's FDA, the European Medicines Agency, Britain's MHRA or India's CDSCO can be a long, cumbersome and frustrating business. Collaborating with an established healthcare corporate might certainly help when it comes to cutting through the red tape, but there are many other factors that could make a conventional partnership arrangement less attractive.

Misunderstandings about key issues like incentives, brand values, rights and responsibilities and decision-making processes can undermine the mutual confidence needed to make a partnership between a large organization and an innovative start-up work smoothly. Both sides need to understand the rules of engagement – and cultural misalignments, personality clashes and disagreements about immediate and longer-term goals can prove fatal. What looks good on paper can quickly become a nightmare.

Before we come to our proposed alternative to the VC, CVC and M&A options, let's briefly discuss a few more approaches that business leaders often like to waste their resources on. They're not asset classes or investment approaches, like M&A, but a series of fashionable and much-hyped ways of passing the time in innovation limbo.

The first example is the start-up accelerator, which aims to support early-stage, growth-driven companies through programmes of education, mentorship and financing. Start-ups enter accelerators for a fixed period of time and as part of a cohort of companies. Today's corporate-owned accelerators have been inspired by the best examples in the outside world, like Y Combinator (which was involved in launching Airbnb and Dropbox) and Techstars. Both have produced some remarkable results. To the best of our knowledge, though, there is not a single corporate accelerator that has delivered results that come anywhere near matching the successes of these rock stars. As far as we know, only one start-up spawned by a corporate accelerator – the Berlin-based mobile bank, N26 – has achieved a valuation of more than $1 billion and reached unicorn status.

Then you have the flashy innovation labs and incubators. These are fantastic for having fun and generating a ton of ideas while people are away from the everyday business that generates income for the company. But what usually happens next is that employees return to their everyday jobs and watch their sparky, transformative ideas slowly die on the vine.

What takes place in innovation labs can be important, but the lab's activities often lack strategic relevance, proper metrics to track success, C-level support and acceptance within the corporate ecosystem. In many cases, those involved in an innovation lab may be unsure whether they're supposed to be serving the core business or disrupting it. And if the process doesn't include thorough market research, listening to customers ad nauseam and systematic testing, there won't be much alignment with real customer needs. But most importantly, without a clear, structured, systematic process and dedicated resources to take these ideas further, this whole endeavour becomes little more than innovation theatre. The resources needed include, at a minimum, board involvement and commitment, access to capital and the kind of realistic and structured entrepreneurial operating model we will be describing below.

Next there are two more approaches to innovation which are neither asset classes nor tools. It's worth mentioning them here, though, because they are often top-of-mind concepts for many business leaders.

First, there are conventional partnerships, often considered to be a powerful way to leverage assets and acquire learning. But what are you expecting to learn? Often, partnerships remain too informal, with little commitment and no proper incentives to achieve success. Partnerships can be helpful, if they are combined strategically with corporate venture building or other asset classes, to serve a specific purpose. Even then, though, they take active work and commitment. Many partnerships are created equal, at least in theory, but few stay that way for long. And you shouldn't be too optimistic about the learning opportunities you'll discover. It is still an us-and-them situation. The companies you are discussing progress with are still not part of your organization, and they won't disclose everything to you. You won't get to hear about the nitty gritty details of their business ups and downs, their team conflicts and their secret problems and fears.

And then, of course, you have internal transformation, which is obviously important for the transition to digitally enhanced operation models and value propositions. But the phrase covers such a multitude of approaches, including process automation, intrapreneurship schemes and culture change programmes, that it doesn't really tell you very much.

The key issue here is that transformation is not just about injecting digital technologies into a company. It is multi-faceted and diffuse, and it's not only concerned with technology. It means changing people, machines and business processes, with all the messiness that entails, and it requires continuous monitoring and intervention from the top to ensure that the right decisions are being made. This is an arduous process that can be important but is unlikely to lead to a massive transformation. And in times of crisis, when companies shift into survival mode, new high-tech initiatives are often the first projects to be shelved, even when they are potentially valuable. If it's done well, though, your internal transformation programme should create a permissive culture for new digital business models and help prepare your core assets for success in new markets.

If you want to create the new normal within your range of impact, innovation labs, corporate accelerators, incubators and CVC won't get you there. They haven't in the past decade, not by a long stretch, and we can't rely on them in moments of existential threat like those we're seeing today. With the current innovation vehicles, you'll be bound to keep coming up short, because the latent potential of your core assets will remain stubbornly untapped, while you dissipate your company's energy in ways that ultimately change nothing. It might feel comfortable and you might glimpse some charming, hopeful ideas, but that's about it.

The real question, though, is: What are the key things you want to have achieved by the end of this decade and how can you align your efforts towards those goals? The residual question, then, becomes: How can we repurpose all our existing assets, from data to technology to networks and any other unfair advantages we may possess, to fuel groundbreaking new digital businesses with a clear economic and social purpose? How can we build the next normal without risking our core business?

Whatever your answers, companies are built in stages, each with its unique challenges and requirements. While there's no cookbook approach to creating something wholly new, you can and must give this process a structure and an enabling governance system that puts the right incentives in place, provides the right level of cultural and operational independence for the team while keeping you in control and systematically minimizes your entrepreneurial risk.

So now, let's talk in practical terms about how you can lead the transition to the new normal.

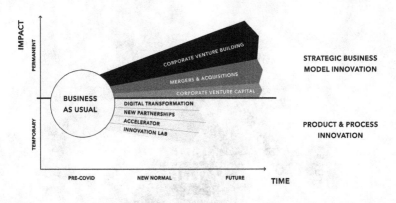

Measures to invent the new normal

Here's our view of how leaders will reinvent their institutions.

CORPORATE VENTURE BUILDING (CVB)

As people keep pointing out in the wake of Covid-19, nothing is ever going to be quite the same again. The new normal, whatever it may turn out to be, will certainly be different.

Economies may eventually recover from the coronavirus disaster, and social life may return to something like its former free and easy state. But the accelerating impacts of climate breakdown will force us to make changes to the way we live and work, even if the next disease pandemic doesn't arrive soon. There will be political changes and behavioural changes, and society's values and priorities may change, too.

That's what you can see in our graphic, above. It's the way corporates, entrepreneurs and markets are going to be interacting for the brief time we can regard as the foreseeable future. It's the new reality, the now reality, the new normal.

The corporate venture building circle

What this illustration emphasizes is the core ingredients for innovation in the next normal – the stuff we need to pay attention to as we take on the big challenges like health and climate.

Business and government leaders need to focus on what that means for businesses and how they can contribute to society in the wake of these tectonic shifts. While many parts of the world are surely heading towards an economic crisis, the survival of most companies will hinge on their ability to adapt to a reality that has been rocked to its foundations. Looking on the bright side, established corporations will find they possess various significant advantages, in the form of their existing assets, that they can now throw into the ring.

Corporate venture building, as a new asset class, is a solution that allows companies to invest in exploiting these existing assets to create differentiating advantages and develop new hybrid business models. But because CVB covers every stage of the venture building process, including capital deployment models, a special kind of governance structure needs to be put in place.

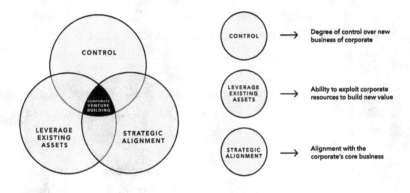

**Corporate venture building
represents a new asset class**

The key advantage of CVB for corporates is that they can jump the entry barriers to play in attractive but difficult, and therefore mostly under-served, markets. If you engage in CVB, however, prepare yourself for an intense relationship, packed with the challenges of different ways of thinking and a different type of team culture. You get more out, and you put more in. It's a real co-creation exercise, and your role in it involves dedicating time, care and attention to the shared journey.

CVB has proved to be especially appropriate for very complex and regulated markets. In these areas, the way you validate your business assumptions and gain early traction is different. Selling clothes, books or electronic goods online is already a formidable challenge, but at least the data models are fairly straightforward, there is little intervention by regulatory authorities and you know there is consumer demand you can benchmark your success against.

As has become obvious by now, hopefully, CVB is particularly suited for industries like healthcare, climate and finance, where there is a complex ecology of forces and factors to take into account.

Alex Manson, the innovation expert from SC Ventures, is clear about the way the different ground rules in heavily regulated industries make it hard to develop new ideas.

"That's the point of creating business models outside the corporate setting that are different from the usual business model," he says.

"Trying them out on the inside would be difficult and too much counter to the organization's nature – not just because of the corporate antibodies, but because the company is not set up to do it. That's why you need to create them outside. Then, when you've created them, you can let them unfold and let them scale, and you've opened up new options for the corporation. But the creation, the incubation, the scaling, the proving the point – all that needs to happen outside, because it's a different kind of set-up."

Being outside, however, does not mean being disconnected. Quite the reverse. As we will see later, the core ingredient for success is a clear strategic governance structure that helps connect and align the new business with the core organization.

Generali Health Solutions' Markus Homann sees governance structure and culture as a linked pair of key success factors.

"To be successful in an area where you don't know all the conditions you will encounter, in a field of ambiguity – which will necessarily be the case if you are innovating – you need a strong culture to hold the project and the people together and to create motivation that goes in one direction."

If the venture breathes in too much of the corporate culture, the chances of success will be put at risk.

"And if you need a strong culture, you need the ability to shape that culture," says Homann. "If you hop from project to project, the culture of the project will be left to chance. It'll depend on the people involved. And it may not have a separate culture, because it will follow the culture of a larger corporation. But you cannot shape it, you cannot develop it and you can't create it."

This is why it's important to take great care choosing the right people and to make sure they have a real vested interest in the long-term viability of the venture, so they can defend that culture against the gravitational pull of the mother ship.

What's needed is the right set-up, a sound governance structure and, of course, a sense of direction. But you are doing something entirely new, by definition, and there are no painting-by-numbers shortcuts to building successful new ventures. The right set-up should inspire you with the trust needed to make bold moves. Boris Marte, Deputy CEO of ERSTE Foundation and head of the bank's innovation hub, sees it the same way, through the lens of his own recent experience.

"Basically, we have a CEO who trusted 25 people he didn't know, all from different industries, with no banking background. But he gave us $15 million and three years – and if you have three years and $15 million and you come up with good ideas, you're going to be able to realize them. I think that's the way to go.

"Creative people need different environments," he says. "Creative people work differently. You have to trust them, trust in creativity."

We've learned that the key ingredients to make this kind of systematic approach work include incentives, culture, connection, regulation and compliance, and impact. And they each encompass three dimensions: corporate, market and entrepreneurs. We've already discussed impact at some length in this book, so now we will look at the other ingredients.

"Corporate venture building needs a clear set of rules, if you're going to create successful cooperation. It is vital to find the right structure in terms of who owns the business and define how key people are incentivized and what the common vision and expectations of the entrepreneurs and the corporate partner are."

SEBASTIAN BOREK
**CEO AND CO-FOUNDER OF
FOUNDERS FOUNDATION**

INCENTIVES

You need to get the incentives right for the people who lead this new business. The key, however, is that your main people are properly incentivized in strict alignment with the overall mission. If you want to get the right people, ensure that they have a significant share in the upside. If you don't, you won't be able to recruit entrepreneurially-minded individuals, because their opportunity costs are simply too high and they'll feel they might as well build a start-up without you in another, less difficult, industry. If you pay a good fixed salary, but nothing else, you'll probably only attract administrators who will meekly decline to challenge you, as long as they get their money.

You must also think of the incentives for your core organization. The worst thing you can do to a young venture is allow it to be hijacked by the interests of particular business units within your corporation. You're not setting out to build an internal digital agency. Make sure that business leaders in the corporation are also incentivized, at least in part, for their contribution to the digital business's stand-alone success, rather than tying their rewards to the success metrics of other business functions.

And, finally, make sure you have the right incentives for the market players to take part. You are probably going to face massive headwinds in the incumbent market. Be sure you have an enticing value proposition for at least some of the existing stakeholders, to secure their support.

CULTURE

Culture eats strategy for breakfast, they say. Be careful how you craft the culture of your ventures. The crucial bit is that the new digital businesses must not be contaminated by a corporate culture that may be functional in its current setting but could be absolutely toxic for the new start-up. As we discussed in depth in Section 4, when we spoke about the ingredients of good entrepreneurship, you need to accommodate different ways of thinking.

There's a catch, however. The cultures on both sides have to be compatible. We've watched in horror as a big healthcare multinational built a new digital business with people from a strong e-commerce background who felt that going to the effort of getting ethics committee approval to speak with cancer patients in hospitals, the prospective customers, was a waste of time. Establishing the quality management systems that were legally required for building software as a medical device was seen as too 'anti-agile' to be worth bothering about. In this case, corporate managers had to step in to protect both the health of the users and the integrity and reputation of the globally-respected parent company.

This was, luckily, a rare and extreme case. But similar challenges may occur even well within the limits of the law. Successful corporate venturers learn to be comfortable with the diverging mindsets, and ways of thinking and judging, that separate entrepreneurs from business leaders. These differences can't just be ignored, so you need to become a translator, to explain things in understandable ways and convince the people you're collaborating with – within their own frames of reference. You need to translate the implications of what you are doing from a finance perspective, from a risk perspective, from a subject matter perspective. Leaving that translation process out will never work. Take them with you on the journey, using step-by-step education and compelling arguments, and you will find you can venture a long way together.

As we will see in our case study about the alley.de app for patients with hip problems, this translation task may require a multi-skilled person like Manuel Mandler, who understands both the language of entrepreneurs and the terms of reference of a big insurance company. The side benefit is that the Mandlers of this world can also connect with the culture of the market they are playing in (the third element in our CVB trifecta). Very few healthcare start-ups can claim to truly understand how companies in the insurance industry function, even though they play such a pivotal role in the sector. Here's to intangible assets!

CONNECTION

Another key component is the web of connections that has to form between the corporation, its emerging digital business, people in the external business environment and staff in the new venture.

The digital business needs to be connected to the corporation in terms of strategy and vision, and have connections to the corporate's core assets. How easy is it for the venture team to access the expertise, data, patents and customer touch-points that belong to the parent company? How useful is the corporation, really, in helping the fledgling business jump all those massive entry barriers that stop competitors entering the market (particularly in highly regulated or complex markets)? In other words, are you really leveraging your unfair advantages through frictionless connections?

The second element is the connection to the market, where again the corporation plays a critical role. How easy is the access to key stakeholders in the market? How strong is the brand in facilitating, or harming, engagement within the industry? How simple is it for the emerging digital business to talk to prospective users? This last point can be particularly problematical in healthcare, where doctors are difficult to reach and patients are often rightly protected from being approached by profit-oriented entities. Having a trusted standing among, or direct access to, the key stakeholders in an industry can provide privileged access to precious insights.

The third element of connection is what happens within the emerging business. As you often need highly diverse teams to succeed in complex industries, you will probably experience the challenges of diversity within your team as well. Diversity is only an advantage if it's managed well and if members of the team are willing to go out of their way to understand each other's points of view, rather than forcing their own way of thinking on them.

REGULATION

As a large corporation in a highly regulated industry, like healthcare, energy or finance, you will face massive restrictions on what you can do, often imposed by competition watchdogs. Make sure that there's no overzealous spillover to the new businesses, which would probably not suffer from too many compliance requirements if they were fully independent entities. But do set clear borders. Then try to be as generous as possible with your existing connections and the expertise that exists within your core workforce. Be really clever about current and upcoming regulations. The era of generic business models is long gone. Regulators have become increasingly aware of the growing power of big tech players and are starting to define new rules. And they are seeing opportunities for human welfare that they want to strengthen.

European Parliament member Eva Kaili sees governments playing a key role in becoming enablers of meaningful innovation.

"Following EU values and the path of respecting fundamental human rights in the digital era, providing tools and making sure people have the time and option to acquire digital skills, and setting global quality standards for governance of data may be our last chance to get it right," she says. "We are impacting positively on the rest of the world, too, and this pandemic has been a catalyst to do that, as it has highlighted the fact of our interconnectivity and interdependence."

The growing interdependence Kaili identifies also affects how we interface with other big companies and platform players. Investing more in building one's own ventures that are already rooted within an industry and backed by a big player means they may stand a better chance of being integrated into the incumbent culture and organization, without losing the can-do growth mentality.

Another manifestation of the crucial role that regulation plays is highlighted in our case study, featured in the previous section, which showed the influence an innovative Estonian entrepreneur was able to wield in helping his government advance its enlightened digital strategies.

PART SCIENCE, PART ART

Now that you know the ingredients, let us share with you how we go about putting them together. There is no straightforward recipe, no simple step-by-step guide for doing this. Frankly, in our own experience, there hasn't been a single instance where we stuck religiously to this path. The circumstances are different each time, because the maturity of the ideas, the set-up and the assets that are available are different every time – and the people, personalities and cultures involved are different, too.

What we can offer, though, is a framework that is solid and practical, and that provides valuable guidance and orientation to refer back to. By bringing all the necessary ingredients together, corporate venture building constitutes a novel asset class that enables organizations to build enterprise value and impact much faster, with less risk, creating a differentiating – maybe even unfair – advantage.

But before we start, there's a health warning.

Boris Marte, the driving force behind Erste Bank's online platform, George, and Deputy CEO of the ERSTE Foundation, has an interesting metaphor for venture building: "When you build a house, the first thing is, you dig a hole for the foundations. You don't start with the roof. People who are not willing to go through all the effort of digging this hole will never build a stable house."

During our interviews for this book, we asked successful entrepreneurs and corporate venturers what it was they wished they'd known before they started building new digital businesses. A surprisingly common answer was: "A thousand things! But I'm happy that I didn't know, because I probably wouldn't have done it."

Building new businesses is incredibly hard. There are so many factors to take into account, most of which are impossible to anticipate. That's why seasoned entrepreneurs and investors are typically unimpressed with 'smart ideas' – to them, great ideas are a commodity. What matters is the execution, driven by the will to suffer through the uncomfortable, even painful, moments that are anything but glorious. Behind the great success stories of shiny start-ups lie long periods of doubt, sleep deprivation, ongoing rejection, pressure and sacrifice.

There is a saying that an entrepreneur is a person who is willing to live a life no one wants, to achieve a life everyone dreams of. What appears easy in these following pages really isn't. But it can be so incredibly rewarding that people keep doing it again and again, often for most of a lifetime.

Managers need to understand that perseverance is crucial. They need to overcome the urge that leads them to cast doubt on anything that doesn't deliver dream results within six to 12 months.

Now, let's get into the three key stages of corporate venture building. The following graphic summarizes them briefly.

CORPORATE VENTURE BUILDING

01	02	03
WHITE SPACE GARAGE	**VALIDATION & EXECUTION**	**SCALE & HARVEST**
Systematic entrepreneurial market analysis for the company in all operating markets	Specification of new digital businesses and sustainable digital venture building process	Maximize portfolio enterprise value through a buy, build, partner approach

PHASE 1: FINDING YOUR WHITE SPACE

KEY MESSAGE

DON'T BUILD BRIDGES IN THE DESERT
When you've got a lot of assets, it's always tempting to use them – 'To the man with a hammer, everything looks like a nail.' Instead, focus first on your customers and find out how you can help them. Make the problem your starting point.

PICK YOUR BATTLES
There are a million problems waiting to be solved out there. Some aren't that pressing. Some already have solutions, or workarounds that people have got used to. A key success factor in the White Space Garage is prioritizing your customer's pains and solving the biggest problems first.

UTILIZE THE SWEET-SPOT MICROSCOPE
You can't be vague any more. All these crazy big ideas that make you sound really smart? Put them away in a drawer. Find the very concrete problem you are going to solve. It may be small, even boring, but you're going to have to know every detail about it.

Corporate venture building is a process of creation, but it is not itself a creative process. It's a combination of factors, bringing together strategy, an entrepreneurial understanding of the market and the corporation's core assets, the investor's insight into broad tectonic shifts in the environment and the essential creativity that's needed to find problems worth solving and systematically develop and test potential solutions for them.

White spaces are a metaphor for areas of high opportunity. They help corporations map out new opportunities to address society's most pressing needs, making them highly relevant from both a strategic and an impact standpoint. The equally metaphorical White Space Garage is the place – or the process – where this search begins. We use this term as a homage to the mythical garages in which so many successful Silicon Valley companies claim to have taken their first baby steps.

But what exactly are these spaces?

They're the spaces, in both new and existing markets, that offer significant potential for new value and impact creation by leveraging new business models and technologies. You'll find three types, as the following graphic shows:

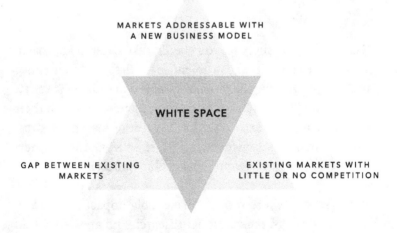

Where can we find white spaces?

Every new digital business starts with an exploration phase. This can be really frustrating, because the deeper you dig, the more you will be confused by the complexities you uncover. It's easy to get lost here. Done right, though, the long days invested in robust, probing research will save you money and grief many times over down the road.

Finding and evaluating white spaces raises the same issues faced by early stage start-ups. It requires both experience and a certain sort of entrepreneurial mindset. What you need to do falls into five stages, as shown in this graphic:

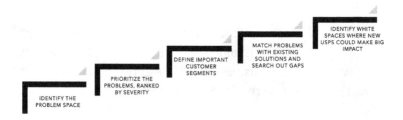

Five steps to find white spaces

Essentially, this suggests you should take a tiered approach. You need to identify the problem space first, and then move towards prioritizing the problems, ranked in order of severity. Next, define important customer segments and match their problems against existing solutions in the search for gaps. That's when you'll uncover the white spaces in which new unique selling points could make a big impact.

White spaces where you can make a big impact are hard to uncover through conventional research and analysis, as all the obvious solutions are probably already being exploited.

To look beyond the obvious, to where the white spaces are hidden and the most impact can be achieved, you need to have the entrepreneur's spirit and curiosity, coupled with an investor's view of the potential (ideally, an impact investor's view).

The hunt for white spaces can be daunting and uncomfortable. Without a genuinely entrepreneurial mindset, you may try, but you'll try in vain. There will be too many risks and too many plausible excuses to stop halfway through the exploration or – just as bad – duck the challenge and settle for a low-ambition business case. That's probably the worst situation of all – half in and half out. We call it 'innovation limbo', and it's not where you want to be.

The crucial thing about the White Space Garage is understanding that this is a deep discovery process. The process requires us to look at things with fresh eyes, without prior assumptions. As childish as it might seem, you have to keep asking both yourself and the people you are interviewing, 'Why?' over and over again – until you reach a stage where you start to see a pattern, gain enough insights and are no longer surprised by what you find.

High-level PowerPoint presentations with snappy titles and minimal bullet points, the staple diet of consultants, are something true entrepreneurs shun.

The era of wild, generic, abstract ideation is over. True invention, nowadays, often has to happen within a tight regulatory corset – and that means you have to know the rules of your industry really well. Don't be afraid of boundaries, though. They're good for the brain. A little bit of resistance will help unleash your creativity.

Let's take a deeper look at this process.

When you start building a new business, the chances are you already have a clear idea of what it is you desire to create. You may even have done some thorough market research beforehand.

The key here is to be humble and treat everything you're tempted to take for granted as a hypothesis that needs to be tested in the real world. What we often see with corporate leaders is that they look at the market through the lens of their company. A pharmaceutical company wanting to use digital to help patients with back pain might think about technologies that help them take their medication properly. But the patients might actually be better served by an exercise app that takes their pain away entirely, removing the need for a drug. One saying you often hear at FoundersLane is 'Let's not build bridges in the desert.' By doing that you can build the perfect solution – and for most corporate leaders, this is probably the easiest exercise. But they underestimate the importance of really understanding the problems that need to be solved.

How confident are you that you really know what the biggest and most painful unmet needs in your market are? Are they, perhaps, the ones you aren't addressing yet?

Don't assume you can mastermind all of this inside your office. At this stage, the biggest thing that stands between you and the success of the business is your own ego.

What's needed here are careful user observations, interviews, analysis of comments on social media and reviews of formal scientific literature, and all the other forms of qualitative research, to uncover both explicit and implicit needs. Blend all this with quantitative research, including surveys and landing page and online marketing analytics, to get a more granular view of who your customers are and which of their problems really need your attention. Allow yourself to be proved wrong as much as possible. It will make your life so much easier later on.

The second big mantra of this phase is 'Pick your battles.' A relentless focus on what matters most is another key to success. Start-ups don't die of starvation, they die of indigestion. All too often, especially in well-funded venture teams, we see people wanting to tackle too many problems at once. This, as it will turn out later, is always a function of underestimating the complexity behind a problem and its possible solutions. Know that you have to focus several times over, on the who, the what, the where and the when.

First comes the *who*. If you look at our Ada Health case study, you will see how the founders first aimed to solve a problem for specialist doctors, then thought that GPs would be the ideal customers, and finally realized that their solution was best suited to solving a common problem that thousands of patients have. It helps to be very granular here. Do away with generic design thinking personas that read more like stereotypes. For example, you might be building an app for people with cancer, but you'll quickly find that no one will want to be reduced to being thought of just as someone suffering from that disease. Aim to understand what really motivates and annoys people, and build a persona that matches different behavioural and cognitive patterns that are relevant to your value proposition.

Then there's the *what*. Essentially, to find out what problems to solve, you need to understand how important they each are and then understand which ones are least effectively met by the current solutions in your market. You will probably be able to narrow that down to about a dozen key issues that you will be able to handle.

The *where* and the *when* seem more trivial, but they can be critical, too. You need to get initial traction, and sometimes that means starting somewhere in the patient journey where you're not necessarily hitting the most interesting market first. But it may be the easiest place to start because it provides you with initial revenues, gives you a first glow of street credibility and creates touchpoints with real customers from which you can learn.

Just be aware that you're rarely dealing with only one stake-holder. Particularly if you are moving into multisided platforms, it should be obvious that you need to charm all the constituents involved in the transactions you're influencing with your technologies.

Also, in the White Space Garage, you must look beyond the obvious. In the alley.de case study, for example, it is noticeable that much of the initial research was conducted far away from the user groups. The research team went through the scientific literature to find out more about the health risks most patients are unaware of. They asked healthcare providers about the most common misconceptions they came across when talking to their patients. When you know those things, you can create moments of surprise for your customers that they will thank you and remember you for. So get that sweet-spot microscope out and put it to work.

We mentioned it before, but just because you've found a clear problem to solve for a clearly defined target group and identified the right starting point, that doesn't mean you'll succeed. The entry barriers – regulatory, cultural, technological or a combination of these, with a host of other challenges – may be prohibitively high. This is where the 'C' (Corporate) element of CVB comes into play.

The question now is about matching your deep market insights with a fresh look at the unfair advantages you can derive from leveraging your existing assets. This, again, requires a humble mindset and a preparedness to be proved wrong. Many corporate leaders overestimate the value of some of their assets, such as access to data or customers. But they may also underestimate the value of other assets that have been unimportant so far but might be extremely useful in the context of this new white space.

As illustrated by the alley.de case study, this can offer you both the chance to create new value and the opportunity to reorient the system towards new goals, including value-based healthcare, thereby defining the new normal for the sector.

So what comes out of it all in the end? The White Space Garage generates a set of initially validated business cases, ready to be presented at board level and hopefully to progress on to venture building.

This is all hard, high-intensity work, but it moves along fast. In our experience, the process that gets you to these results takes around eight weeks and usually requires roughly 80 research interviews. Trying to do it all in less than four weeks is physically and mentally impossible – and the impossible is something we try not to recommend.

The true payoff from the White Space Garage process is hugely reduced uncertainty. You will come out of it with a better understanding of where the most under-served problems lie and have a clearer idea of the solutions that will best meet these needs in the light of all the regulatory, technological, cultural and market constraints you're up against. And you will have gained clarity on where your core assets might play the biggest role in developing an unfair advantage. In practice, we have often seen corporate leaders totally change their understanding of their core assets. Some unfair advantages may turn out to have been completely overestimated and have near zero intrinsic value in the new context, or they may just be hard to mobilize. On the other hand, some new ones may appear that had not previously been recognized at all.

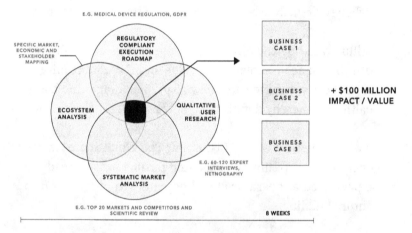

White space garage deliverables

The illustration above highlights the core domains that are subject to deep analysis in CVB. Alongside the user research mentioned above, they include an analysis of the ecosystem, including its specific economic logic, such as intrinsic market failures, a systematic market analysis that looks at the competitive landscape and the body of scientific knowledge affecting the domain. The top circle stands for the regulatory compliance execution roadmap. In complex industries, this goes far beyond most other strategy documents. It usually contains detailed analysis of the various implications that regulation may have for the venture's potential launch strategy.

We all have limited resources, and opportunity costs are high. So it makes sense to focus on whatever offers the highest potential impact.

If you go for one high-impact venture every ten months, you stand a very good chance of achieving a value of $100 million within five years. That's if you get the next steps right as well, of course. Within just eight weeks, this White Space Garage allows you to identify the opportunities to generate massive value through detailed, risk-reduced business models.

However, knowing what is good enough is an imperfect science. It's like motor racing. The driver can have all the performance data and all the input from the engineers, but still know, from experience, that the car is not quite behaving as it should, whatever the numbers say.

If you were an investor who was unable to develop a feel for the numbers and was risk averse by instinct, you would probably have said no to every one of the start-up ideas and business models that have gone on to take their place among today's best-known billion-dollar-plus unicorns. They weren't funded by corporates, any of them – almost certainly because of the large number of different ways they could have failed before they broke through to enjoy success.

PHASE 2: VALIDATION AND EXECUTION

KEY MESSAGE

KILL YOUR DARLINGS

Phase 2 is the time to put all your vanity away and look for trouble. Seek to have your assumptions demolished. This is the business equivalent of the scientist's systematic experiments in the pursuit of truth.

NO PLACE FOR INNOVATION THEATRE

Don't be satisfied with a proof of concept. Corporate venture building is about making things people want, at scale. It's not enough just to prove your idea might find some buyers. Executing it and establishing a new normal is what counts.

WHO YOU ARE IS WHAT YOU DO

This is going to hurt. The team you pick in the early days will lay crucial foundations for your mission. But you'll probably find that some of the people you hoped would be star performers have the wrong skills or the wrong mindset. Be ready to take tough decisions.

GET YOUR INCENTIVES STRAIGHT

Everyone needs to be aligned and incentivized: the founding team of the New Value Organization, the key team of the core organization, and the team that provides the relevant assets.

Great job! You're showing you have the humility to be proved wrong hundreds of times, and to be rejected by many potential customers until you find someone who's willing to talk to you.

Congratulations on your long nights spent going over and over your analysis and coping with your ongoing confusion and debates. You have done your very best to get all the information you could get, pieced it together thoughtfully and gone on to craft a careful programme for execution. Here is your bulletproof plan. Well... not really.

Now the time has come to kill your darlings. Let's return to that metaphor about building a house. Being willing to dig that hole for the foundations is important. Conducting thorough research to figure out if you really need a house there at all, before you start, is intelligent. Thinking that successful execution will now come naturally is ignorant. You might hit bedrock or power cables on the way. The walls might be leaking water or you might simply run out of money halfway through the process.

In short, it's time to let your plan meet reality. The worst thing you can do at this stage is to say: "I've done my research. Now all I need is to put the requirements I've uncovered into a Gantt chart and wait till the perfect product is ready." We've seen many companies starting to hire an oversized team to meet all the anticipated demand, well before there's any proof that this demand actually exists. This is dangerous. As precious as your work until now has been, you still have a long way to go until you can safely move up to be an established company. There are still risks.

What seem like good ideas may not match up with the realities of the customer journey – or certain stages of it. They may be too expensive or too risky, if you try to apply them to the whole market. So you may need to start small or start in a very specific customer segment, and then scale up and outwards to others. You need to find out where the sweet spot is. Where can you begin to implement your theoretical ideas and bring them to life?

At this stage there is no way of knowing what talents you are eventually going to need, other than your core team of entrepreneurially-minded leaders, who pretty much live and breathe the mindset outlined in Section 4.

You need to incentivize them appropriately, so that they have a true interest in helping your organization grow big over the next few years, rather than just satisfying your reporting needs.

Much of what you do in this phase will remind you of what you did in the White Space Garage. But where you emerged before with low-fidelity prototypes and mock-ups, now you will be doing it with increasingly mature products. Where you previously walked out to interview 80 people about your new idea, you will be doing that again, now, to find out about their willingness to pay.

Everything becomes more serious, but you maintain your iterative approach, inching forward, step by step. With each discovery you make, you adapt the specifications of your initial idea ever so slightly. Maybe you even do a major pivot, if the evidence strongly suggests you should.

The aim should be to achieve a sufficient level of confidence in each of these areas. But it's unlikely you will achieve 100% certainty. Residual risks will remain, and others will only show up later on. You can't hope to solve every single problem or mitigate every risk at this stage. What this means in practice will depend on the particular circumstances. In one situation – in the medical space, for instance – it might be enough to have a single clinic as your initial partner. In another, you might need to be working with hundreds of end-users before you can assume you have a scalable consumer model.

The key here is to balance learning and pitching. During the White Space Garage, the most important thing was to maximize for learning. Now, you also have to start to convince people to buy in to your vision. Much like a seed stage start-up, you'll be hunting for Letters of Intent or first customers. These will probably be typical early adopters who have already been looking for a solution to the problem you are devoting your energies to. They will generally be patient with you and their comments will help you ripen the product further.

But the time will come when you want to reach a wider spread of customers. You will have to understand how to cater for their needs as well, which will often be very different from those of your early customers. Again and again, learning and iterating is the core theme of this second phase. The key difference is that the level of complexity involved is gradually increasing.

In multisided businesses, this is even more complicated. You suddenly have to appeal to different user groups simultaneously – and their needs may contradict each other. That may require a bit more creative thinking on your part. The founders of alley.de, for example, found a clever way of focusing on the different problems that affected both sides of the platform. The team realized that doctors would appreciate having a dashboard that brought together all the relevant information about their patients and discovered ways to make aggregating all that data equally attractive and desirable for patients, too.

There are also macro trends that can suddenly change your value proposition. Many healthcare start-ups have strengthened their focus on telemedicine, for example. Doktor24, another of our case studies, knew straight away that it already had most of the assets needed to deliver safe Covid-19 tests during the pandemic, and it quickly become one of the key players in that field. Listening closely to your market is important, too, in less obvious cases. You will constantly have to reassess demand, and your supply, and reprioritize your activities while sticking to old promises.

Little by little, you will establish partnerships with key players in the field, eventually gaining some who will become volunteer co-creators. In one venture, Sven even found practising doctors who were willing to accompany him to important ethics committee meetings, to endorse him as a trusted voice in the field and help to push a new and potentially disruptive technology. Trust is critical in the early stages, when you have no track record – and you may be able to 'borrow' it, as Sven did.

As your concepts ripen, you will potentially need to create a new company, register your products with the authorities (maybe getting CE or FDA approval for medical software), establish a quality management system and slowly begin to hire new talents. To make it even more complicated, early stage companies are fluid and unpredictable, so the people you need now may not be the people you'll need in six months' time.

In fact, your organizational structure – the team, the tech capabilities, the access to corporate assets, everything that will be needed to make this business happen – is another key risk factor. This can put you on a very steep learning curve. In healthcare, for example, your well-honed business case may make it look easy, until you start to dig into the details. But the more you look, the more you see the complexities and regulatory constraints. It's a market that requires a lot of expertise and operational knowledge to avoid the pitfalls, and you need team members who know what can and can't be done.

At this stage you need to be extremely careful with the culture you are crafting in any new digital business. As highlighted in Section 4, you need different mindsets. Having too many managers who aren't used to the entrepreneurial approach can lead to the premature death of the business. Oliver Schoeller, the new CEO of Gothaer Insurance, was constantly in the know and accepted changes of focus, allowing his spin-off, alley.de, to shape its own destiny. In meetings, Schoeller acted as a sounding board, adding real value but also signalling his continuing faith in Manuel Mandler, alley's CEO, and his ability to fashion a culture tuned to the new venture's needs and aspirations.

KEY SUCCESS FACTORS FOR THE INCUBATION PHASE OF THE CVB MODEL

So what else is needed to make this a success? You also need the right set-up, as shown in the following graphic.

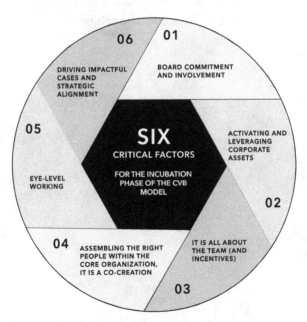

The essentials for corporate venture building success

This starts with dependable buy-in by the corporate board and direct access to it. The leaders of the new business must have a voice in the boardroom to discuss challenges at eye level. The second component, as discussed earlier, is the activation of existing assets within the corporation. Then you'll need an adequate team set-up, with clear responsibilities divided between the entrepreneurs and the corporate team, that covers the broad range of skills needed. A critical success factor that we increasingly came to appreciate is having an internal champion with deep insights into the situation and the ability and respect within the organization to do the job of 'translating'. This person must be able to act as an advocate for the new digital business and help it navigate through the corporation's culture and access key assets. At the same time, this internal champion can help the core organization assimilate learnings from the New Growth Organization. Last but not least, the whole team should start with a clear focus and a shared vision of what is to be achieved.

A VALUE-BASED PLATFORM

What do you get when you mix strategic vision and strong curiosity? Ambition for constant improvement and drive towards innovation? You get Oliver Schoeller and Manuel Mandler, a team capable of developing a new kind of data-driven healthcare platform. Schoeller is now CEO of Gothaer, one of Germany's biggest mutual insurance groups, with sales of €4.7 billion and over 4.1 million members. Mandler, former CDO of Gothaer Krankenversicherung AG, is the founder and CEO of alley.de, an up-and-coming value-based health-care platform that aims to establish new sustainable quality standards in healthcare.

Mandler is the type of corporate venturer we described earlier in this book. He's a man who has continuously reinvented himself throughout his life, and has just recently stepped out of his senior leader-ship position at Gothaer Health Insurance to become the founder of alley.de, Gothaer's first digital spin-off. Mandler is still deeply involved in a Europe-wide network of health insurers and is a mentor at the Euro-pean Institute of Technology. To him, it's becoming increasingly obvious that there is an urgent need for health systems to move towards value-based health-care, an important concept we've already discussed in Section 3 of this book.

Getting there is no easy undertaking, though, as it requires massive shifts in the foundations of the health-care system to unleash its full potential. And it means moving beyond the biomedical box, looking at social determinants of health (such as nutrition, environment, education and household income) as well. This is becoming urgently needed as changing demographics and other cost drivers are threatening the sustainability of today's health and care systems.

"Transition from an output-based to an outcome-based health and care system starts with making the right data available to patients, providers and payers," Mandler explains. "This is not just a technological problem. It's primarily about deciding what data to collect and ensuring that it is of high quality and kept updated."

Patients are asked a series of carefully chosen questions and receive help in aggregating all the healthcare documents they have, so that alley.de can create a personalized health profile of each user. It can then offer tailored patient education and exercise advice and provide all the information the patient's care providers may need. Alley.de is becoming a personal companion for people with hip pains and osteoarthritis, from the first symptoms to successful treatment and beyond, with the aim of improving patients' safety, autonomy and quality of life.

When Mandler launched the new venture, he had already done a lot of research and reached a deep understanding of what his goals should be. Now the time had come to let the hypothesis meet reality. He and his team spoke to over 100 doctors, nurses, physiotherapists and patients. They browsed through social media comments by patients with hip problems, attended orthopaedics conferences and patient information events at hospitals and even booked appointments on Doctolib, a mobile scheduling service for health practitioners, to get face-to-face time with the relevant people in the field (paying the doctors for the privilege).

IMPACT
They quickly realized that many of the initial assumptions made perfectly logical economic sense, but were entirely misaligned with the incentives and regulations of today's healthcare system.

For example, one key assumption was that bringing doctors more patients would be a value driver, as higher volumes would increase revenue. But in Germany, volumes per doctor are capped, benchmarked historically against the previous year and against a doctor's peers. A family doctor who suddenly sees many more patients might end up doing it at her own expense. Instead, many doctors showed an interest in having better prepared patients ahead of operations, because it would save time wasted on mundane information-seeking tasks like making phone calls, getting discharge letters faxed and so on. And they were soon convinced that alley.de would also empower patients to become more active contributors to their own treatment, leading to better outcomes.

Understanding where the real impact lies is no easy task. Instilling the principles of value-based healthcare in a system that operates on very different principles can easily get confusing for agile product development teams. The problem is that it's an approach that looks at all areas of human life, including the environment. It's all too easy to get lost in the complexities.

Alley.de had to prioritize the problems it should focus on by finding the most important unmet needs of both patients and healthcare providers. If they catered to only one side of the equation, the other side would probably sabotage it. If you build the greatest solution for patients, but doctors need to put in extra hours to make it work, they are going to hate your solution.

In the search for the right impact at the right moment in the customer journey, the team really went through the painful details. It was a joy to watch. Within the first few weeks, the initial customer journey, as mapped on the office wall, grew from one A1 page, to two, to four, and eventually to six pages — with new insights emerging with every update.

CONNECTIONS

But Mandler, being a healthcare insider himself, knew that just having a great product wouldn't cut it. And he was well aware of the importance of having the right connections within the system. "The first step is to build trusted networks with the care providers who are leaders in quality. Then you have to get other players involved, as you gradually aim to drive systemic change," he says. On top of this, thanks to his long and successful career in the parent group, Mandler was ideally suited to the job of keeping close ties going with Gothaer's senior management.

CULTURE

Alley.de frequently returned to prospective users with simple prototypes, sometimes just on paper, to illustrate the features and design of its proposed solution.

The doctors loved that it was innovative, but respected the existing system. Alley.de was relying on established, proven measurements and questionnaires and it provided guidance based on the latest research and well recognized guidelines.

As a result of alley.de's foundations in evidence-based healthcare practices and its highly trained, diverse team, it managed to win support from key opinion leaders in the field within the first few months of the company's existence. Seasoned orthopaedic surgeons can be tough individuals to convince, but one of them soon coined the term 'grown-up start-up' when referring to alley.de's businesslike approach.

And while alley.de took some members of the parent company on board, it also carefully chose outsiders who would bring in a different vibe, so the new company could shape a new culture while still remaining compatible with that of the core business.

REGULATION

There's another layer of complexity: healthcare's heavy regulation. Alley.de had to register three software tools as medical devices with the German authorities, and managed to do it in little more than six months from the company's launch. The IT team used to talk about two 'monsters' which were always represented by grisly cartoon characters in their PowerPoint presentations: Data Protection and Medical Device Regulation.

But the clear value proposition the team had developed during its White Space Garage effort was truly helpful for the regulatory work as well. Gothaer's board was also canny enough to not superimpose unnecessary regulatory constraints on its new digital business.

Given alley.de's founding team's strong background in healthcare, they knew already that 'Move fast and break things' was not going to cut much ice here. Instead, they carefully researched the existing scientific literature, made robust user safety plans and ended up saving a lot of money by avoiding costly mistakes. Thinking things through allowed them to anticipate dangers and find evidence about which features would be likely to work and which would not.

INCENTIVES

Alley.de would not have been possible without the right people. It was always going to take someone like Mandler, who was willing to give up the security of a senior leadership position to step into an unproven business model like alley.de. And it was always going to need senior executive support, too. As Mandler emphasizes, this would not have been possible without the wholehearted and intelligent backing of the parent company's boss, Oliver Schoeller: "He takes audacious steps. He's more of a Steve Jobs or an Elon Musk than a typical insurance company CEO. He dares a lot. His mindset is rare in the insurance space."

Alley.de knows there's still a long road ahead. "This is not an investment that focuses on the exit after three or four or five years," Schoeller explains. "It is a strategic investment, but we decided to start building alley.de on our own. We'll be looking for other investors, and every player is potentially welcome to join. But we're not seeking quick cash; we're looking for other strategic investors.

"We are convinced that you need a strategic investment for this type of business model. So it's a long-
lasting investment. The response of the market is too
slow, much too slow. Even with a swift market entry, you
need at least five to seven years to really be a crucial
part of the entire system."

Alley.de is in it for the long run. It takes patience, but
the stakes are high – for the patients, for the doctors
and for Gothaer and its healthy, bouncing spin-off.

PHASE 3: SCALE AND HARVEST

KEY MESSAGE

SCRUTINIZE COMPULSORY OPTIONS
A frequent question is, 'Should we do it all ourselves or buy or partner?' In practice, you will usually have to do all three, at one stage or another. The real question is: What should your core activity be?

LET GO, MOSTLY
You've got to learn to let go – but not let go completely. While making due allowance for pivots and trusting the entrepreneurial team to execute smartly, you'll still need to keep a close eye on the strategy, to ensure alignment and to be sure there's a sounding board available when the going gets tough.

MAKE THE MODEL WORK FOR YOU
Have an operating model in place that ensures you are able to act fast. Any delay in getting hold of pre-agreed follow-up funding or access to core assets can put the digital business at risk.

REDEFINE YOUR UNFAIR ADVANTAGES

We've done the heavy lifting. We have a product or service that's commercially validated in terms of interest and willingness to pay. We also have assets that give us the right to play and win in the market, a team to run the new digital business, and the investment funding needed to take the next steps.

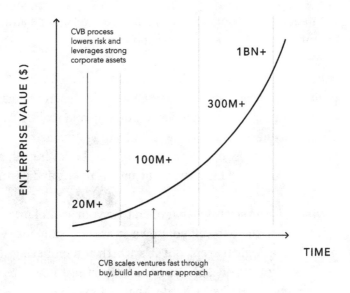

ENTERPRISE VALUE ($)

CVB process
lowers risk and
leverages strong
corporate assets

1BN+

300M+

100M+

20M+

TIME

CVB scales ventures fast through
buy, build and partner approach

Corporate venture building for rapid growth

It is time to scale the business before we can harvest. Scaling means we need to grow the business, which probably means hiring more people. You don't want to kill a winning culture, but getting ready for scaling may need adjustments to the culture and attitudes that got the company to where it is today. New branches may need to be opened, and expansion to new countries may need to be led. More partners may need to be signed. External communication needs to be professionalized and aligned. And there are many more complexities involved in scaling. Growing revenues from $1 million to $10 million is a different kind of task from starting from scratch and getting sales up to $1 million for the first time. It takes different techniques and disciplines, possibly even different personalities. This is one of the many points in the development of the new venture where it helps enormously to have constructive input from the board and the chance to discuss and test your ideas with people who understand what needs to be done and are committed to the shared goals and strategy.

With corporate venture building, we are not in the same position as a typical start-up. The CVB model ensures a smaller element of risk when it comes to building and scaling a new digital business. This privileged advantage stems from the fact that assets from the corporation can be leveraged, and can be used to provide us with the means to buy and partner.

Buying existing start-ups that operate in your area of interest, and tailoring them to suit your own strategic vision, may well be the next logical step. But it's worth remembering that successfully acquiring, merging and integrating founder teams and companies is always harder than it looks.

Your chances of getting this right go up significantly if you understand what you are buying and how to operate it well. CVB ensures this through continuous validation and revalidation of customer problems, solutions, markets, talent sourcing and the use of unfair assets from the inside out.

The more you know about the business you're in, the more likely you are to make successful acquisitions. Your own experience provides strategic awareness about the market opportunities and how they should be approached. You will be learning, all the time, about the skills, assets and mindset that are needed to execute and grow in these markets. So the best way to ensure that future acquisitions will work well is to execute and grow your own new digital business first.

As the Solytic case study illustrates, this will help you target the right assets to acquire and make it much easier to reduce post-merger risk by correctly aligning the incentives between different founder teams and the core business. Being able to show a detailed understanding of the business model and key success factors of a business you want to acquire will also greatly increase the likelihood of the acquisition target team accepting your offer. For Solytic, acquisitions led to accelerated growth and access to new countries and enhanced the data foundation to fuel new machine learning-based features. The individuals involved will value your experience and see you as a respected partner beyond the limited partnership implied by your financial capabilities.

Companies that are thinking about the investments needed for corporate venture building should realize that they don't necessarily have to finance everything themselves. But if they lead the early rounds, which are usually perceived to involve the biggest risks, other investors will be that much more enthusiastic about participating. The required capital will be available faster this way, enabling the founding team to tackle the opportunity with more confidence.

Another option that can be leveraged to scale the new digital business is partnering. You have not fully developed your product yet and, as a result, you are likely to partner with companies in the value chain close to you.

But whatever you do on your journey to grow the venture, the most important lessons are:

1. Let go, mostly. A core ingredient for success is the ability to let go... but not entirely. While you should allow for pivots and trust that the execution will go well, you should always keep a close eye on the overall strategy. This will ensure alignment and be a precious sounding board for your entrepreneurial team. Within business and beyond,

we must not underestimate the role of communication. The sounding board function avoids any disconnect between the corporate strategy and the new digital business's direction. A disconnect can grow unnoticed right up to the point where it will be too late, when the disconnect in strategy is too big and the justification to continue together becomes weak. The sounding board ensures not just solid communication but the sustainability of the relationship itself.

2. Make sure you have a realistic operating model in place that will enable you to act fast. Every delay in getting your hands on pre-agreed follow-up funding or arranging access to core assets can put the digital business at risk. On the journey of scaling you will encounter many surprises, probably more than you'd wish for. There are plenty of useful books about this, such as *The Hard Thing About Hard Things*, by Ben Horowitz, which we would certainly recommend you to read.

The objective of this phase is to scale the new digital business for the new normal as fast as possible. You can optimize here for revenue, profit, social impact or valuation. Or, alternatively, you can aim for a combination of those. This needs to be aligned with the specific objectives of CVB, your board and your stakeholders.

All of this will ensure that CVB is used to its full potential and that venture scaling can take place in close cooperation with the corporation, making full use of its assets. If your irrigation system leaks, it's not well connected and it is operated infrequently, what kind of a harvest can you expect? Without proper irrigation and scaling, there won't be much to harvest. On the other hand, with proper irrigation, good water management and a well connected system, the harvest will be plentiful and the yield from the new growth may eventually overtake the traditional crop, to become even bigger and more significant in its impact.

THE HYBRID ORGANIZATION

The ultimate goal of all this activity is to create an organization that is able to protect, optimize and expand its core business, while generating enough dynamic new businesses, products and services to position it for success in a fast-changing and largely unpredictable world.

That can't be done without investing in the new normal, taking some risks and trying a spread of initiatives, some of which are bound to fail. But this kind of innovation activity is virtually impossible within the body of a traditional corporation. The processes, habits, KPIs, skills and leadership mindset that are suitable for the steady, incremental growth and meticulously efficient execution that characterize large and well-run businesses are simply not appropriate for start-up operations, especially those involving digital technologies and new business models. Even the traditional departmental structure, where staff sit in separate units defined by a function such as sales, engineering, production, marketing or HR, acts as a barrier to fast action and holistic thinking about new business opportunities and customer needs.

Something different is needed: an infusion of new blood, new ideas and awareness of new possibilities.

The standard response to this problem is to recruit someone dynamic (maybe with the title of Chief Digital Officer), to hire consultants, to embark on a flurry of staff training programmes focused on design thinking and agile development or to look for acquisitions that can bring the desired digital skills and entrepreneurial talents into the company.

We've all seen how far short these efforts tend to fall. Unfortunately, CDOs aren't usually given the power, prestige and autonomy they would need to make a real difference, and they often become disillusioned and leave without having achieved much. Training programmes can be quite inspirational on the day, but generally lose their impact as soon as staff return to their usual roles. And promising, energetic start-ups quickly lose momentum, and often personnel, as they're sucked into the routines, disciplines and conventions of a large and hierarchical corporation.

The answer to these problems, if you can achieve it, is to create a structure known as a hybrid organization. The term refers to a company that is equally adept at managing today's business and adapting to future needs – one that's able to balance the exploitation techniques needed for efficient day-to-day operations with the exploration skills and mindset required to develop new ideas and new business models. In reality, of course, hybrid organizations that can successfully balance present and future needs are roughly as rare as unicorns.

This combination of qualities is precious indeed, as most companies are far better at dealing with today's demands. Some are conspicuously good at discontinuous innovation. Few are capable of juggling both exploitation and exploration, mainly because hybrid leaders, with talents in both areas, are extremely hard to find. We need them very much, both to help modernize our businesses and realign them with the realities of the new post-Covid world, and also to shake up our politics and drive collaborative efforts to spur the world into immediate and determined action on climate change.

THE ENTREPRENEURIAL
OPERATING MODEL

The practical framework that enables you to create a successful hybrid organization is known as the Entrepreneurial Operating Model. This is another of the key ingredients needed to develop your response to the new normal.

Versatility in business doesn't just happen. The hybrid organization is the key to making it work. You have to construct an organization that's shaped and structured to encourage people to think about today's actions and tomorrow's consequences at the same time. That isn't easy. If you are usually focused on exploitation, like almost all big companies, the best way to do it is to create an organization, closely linked to but not within the company, that is specifically charged to define, validate and scale the opportunities presented by our progress towards the new normal.

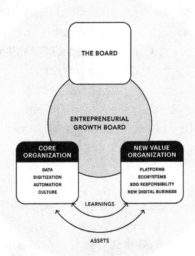

Entrepreneurial operating model

In the diagram above, the core organization is shown on the left-hand side. This is your traditional business, optimized for efficiency, disciplined, consistent and, if it doesn't respond to the changes in the world around it, potentially vulnerable to disruption.

On the right is the new venture, the New Value Organization. It's optimized for new growth and responsible for sowing the seeds that will grow into new businesses and, if all goes well, guaranteeing the continuing relevance and prosperity of the business as a whole.

These two units are obviously going to be very different in size at first. But it is essential that the New Value Organization is seen as being just as important as the core business unit, that it reports in directly to the CEO and that it is understood that its activities must always in some way be relevant to the overall strategy and future of the organization.

In the middle of the Entrepreneurial Operating Model, and forming the essential connection between the two units, is the Entrepreneurial Growth Board (EGB). This is the vital link that makes sure that requirements and learning, assets and information can be transferred back and forth between the two. It is essential to make corporate board members part of the EGB to ensure strategic alignment and optimal resource allocation.

The Entrepreneurial Operating Model is there to provide you with a clear framework to enable you to drive corporate venture building in the best possible way. It is an important structure, in itself, and it has the function of ensuring that communication between the corporation and the new digital business is clear, frank and unambiguous. In fact, the EOM has to be a bilingual entity. It must understand the corporation's structure and concerns and speak its language, while being equally fluent in putting across the ideas coming out of the venture.

Boris Marte, Erste Group's deputy CEO and head of the bank's innovation hub, sees paying attention to the job of translating ideas between the corporation and the new venture as one of the keystones of effective innovation.

"People need to question themselves," he says. "The first step in innovation is inventing the right questions. If you're not ready to question yourself, every conversation will just be superficial. It needs lots of translation to make sure everyone's speaking the same language. It takes a lot of management attention to be successful."

The Entrepreneurial Growth Board takes the strategic decisions and acts as a steering committee. And, yes, in this book we have simplified the EGB as one board. In some corporate organizations it needs to be more than one board in order to meet compliance requirements. It governs how and when the New Value Organization can leverage the assets of the core organization and enables knowledge sharing between the two organizations, as exemplified by the arrows. It also has the authority to make the crucial buy/build/partner and invest decisions that may well determine the pace and direction of future progress.

Especially in these turbulent times, we must aim to streamline all our innovation activities to guarantee getting the best performance we can, in terms of strategic alignment, resource allocation, cross-effects and speed.

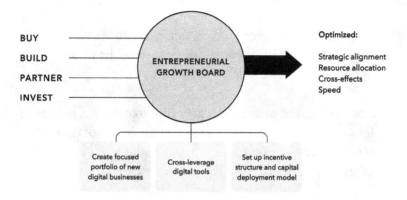

Streamline innovation activities

A formally established Entrepreneurial Growth Board helps you coordinate and align all your new growth endeavours. Among other things, it needs to answer important questions like:

- What are the KPIs, milestones and decision gates your New Value Organization will work to?

- What representatives from the core business need to be in the EGB and/or connected with the New Value Organization in order to ensure positive cross-effects and maximum leverage of assets and speed?

- How do we make sure there will be fertile cross-pollination between the core business and the New Value Organization and its new digital businesses, in terms of insights, skills and assets?

- Which new areas are strategically relevant and attractive?

As speed is always one of the key factors in the development of new digital businesses, these are crucial decisions. If the team has spotted a white space opportunity, signalling a genuine gap in the market where there is no direct competition – or if there is the chance of acquiring a company whose skills, business model, technology or customer base could catapult the new business ahead – the decision to go for the acquisition option may be of major strategic importance.

eBay, for example, was already well established and growing fast when it stepped in to buy PayPal. PayPal had just IPOed in February 2002, but eBay saw the great strategic advantage for its C2C and B2C sales of owning a fast and trusted payment service. Backing its strategic judgement, it was willing to pay $1.5 billion, 77% above the IPO price, in July 2002.

More often, though, the New Value Organization will be focusing on building new ventures or partnering with other specialized companies with complementary skills or assets. The Entrepreneurial Growth Board needs to assess and approve the right route for each particular project and its make-up has to reflect the range and complexity of the assessments and policy decisions it will have to make.

Because of its crucial role as the bridge between the two organizations, as shown in the Entrepreneurial Operating Model, the Entrepreneurial Growth Board should always include at least one representative of the board, ideally the CEO, as a member. A good indicator of focus is how much time a board member dedicates to this. Don't expect to build a New Value Organization for a large corporation if a board member is going to invest less than 10% of his or her time. The EGB also needs to include the appropriate top-level managers from the New Value Organization, someone from strategy or finance (or both) and a representative of the core organization's innovation efforts. And to ensure it is realistically sympathetic to the need to build the New Value Organization quickly and sustainably, which will often be digital-related, it also needs to include the balancing voices of at least two experienced external digital leaders with as much hands-on experience as possible of building and scaling digital businesses. Of course, besides the sharing of experience, this is also about ensuring that the EGB is focusing on impact and not on political discussions.

The EGB is there to defend the New Value Organization when it comes under pressure, to set goals and metrics, to monitor the venture portfolio and to keep the organization and its activities on track.

Its members carry the ultimate responsibility for the successful implementation of the corporate venture building process, and they must be prepared to act as sounding boards for ideas, as critical investors and as ambassadors, carrying the message about the unit's activities to other parts of the organization.

A well-run Entrepreneurial Growth Board also fulfils an important educational role in relation to the main corporate board. Its reports to the board, or the dedicated board members' reports to their peers, on the progress of the New Value Organization and on specific ventures help ensure that those at the top of the organization develop an understanding of the key concepts and practices in the world of digital platforms, ecosystems and technologies. As these ideas start to gain traction, they tend to prompt the wider cadre of senior executives to start thinking differently about the larger part of the corporation and edging towards playing a full role in the development of a newly capable and versatile hybrid organization.

IT'S EASY TO GET IT WRONG

The shape of the Entrepreneurial Operating Model, with the Entrepreneurial Growth Board as the bridge in the middle, is a tried and tested format that needs to be adhered to.

It is vital, for example, that the New Value Organization does not report in to any part of the core organization, as it must be free to work in a different way, with wholly different expectations about timescales and risk.

As one of our corporate partners pointed out to us recently, without this strictly enforced separation, the New Value Organization will always be vulnerable to every round of cost-cutting within the core business. With longer horizons and, in all probability, little in the way of short-term revenue, it is just a sitting duck whenever savings and cost-cutting are called for. As a result, it is advisable to have a dedicated capital deployment model in place.

"If you suddenly have a cost reduction programme, it's very easy to say 'Let's stop this new stuff,' because this money hasn't been spent yet and we don't see immediate results," our partner said. "You have to treat it outside the core business in order not to kill it off as the first thing that goes."

Ideally, the Entrepreneurial Operating Model should receive at least 10% of the time resources of the core organization's top level management.

The aim of the New Value Organization is to build the new normal with a portfolio of digital businesses that are relevant to the strategic aims of the overall business, that the overall business can control, and that can accelerate the ability of the organization to achieve its ultimate mission.

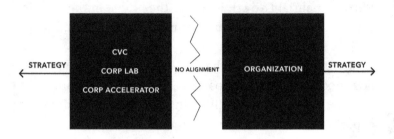

The problem is misalignment

The methods used could involve buying, building, partnering and leveraging all kinds of internal innovation vehicles, such as corporate accelerators, corporate innovation labs and the like, depending on what is most appropriate. The ultimate objective is usually that the digital business in this portfolio should have the potential to grow to become as valuable as the whole of the current business. (Imagine creating a Doktor24 if you were a large healthcare provider, or N26 if you were a large retail bank.) But that's not always the goal. Sometimes the strategic value of a new venture may be essentially defensive, to counter a move by a competitor, establish a bridgehead in a developing market or secure control points that provide access to key customers. Strategy, after all, can often be about positioning the business, rather than capturing short-term profits, and different elements in a digital portfolio may have different roles to play in creating the conditions for future success.

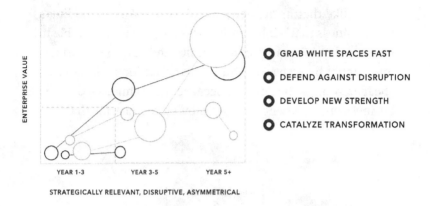

GRAB WHITE SPACES FAST

DEFEND AGAINST DISRUPTION

DEVELOP NEW STRENGTH

CATALYZE TRANSFORMATION

ENTERPRISE VALUE

YEAR 1-3   YEAR 3-5   YEAR 5+

STRATEGICALLY RELEVANT, DISRUPTIVE, ASYMMETRICAL

Fast-track learning: portfolio of ventures

But how the ventures come into being and develop is very different from the way the core business works. Most development projects in the core organization still work on the traditional waterfall principle, with everything planned out in sequential stages – typically conception, initiation, analysis, design, construction, testing, deployment and maintenance – and each phase only starting when the previous one is completed.

The classic waterfall plan goes something like this. If I want to build a factory in India, I look at our previous experience in Mexico. I work out that it will take a year to build and six months more to go live, with all the people, structures, marketing and global integration in place. Then we'll start to get the production lines working and the first revenues in and we'll move into profit in the third year.

That's how most corporates work. And it makes sense, for activities that are genuinely that predictable. You do it to plan, make it work and optimize everything down to the last decimal point.

It's not like that in the new, digital world. You're building a new business that's inherently unpredictable and unstable in its early days. Progress comes in fits and starts, sometimes interrupted by setbacks. And no plan that looks three years ahead is going to be any use, because the technology and the business environment are both moving too fast for that.

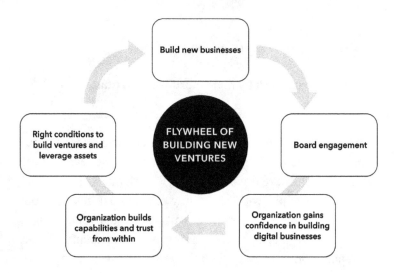

The key to growing a successful business against this sort of background is responsiveness and a deep understanding of customer behaviour and customer needs. Behaviours are changing fast – look at the way young people now actually prefer to make bookings or arrangements via an app rather than by making a phone call, even if the call would be quicker. The only way to ensure you make what customers need is to engage with them continuously and respond fast, so you build what they want while they still want it.

You can have a solus position in an attractively untapped digital market at the beginning of the year and find that by August there's a new company squatting in that space, one that someone's backed with $10 million. If the Entrepreneurial Growth Board agrees with your assessment and approves of the logic, you can buy that company and possibly be alone again in the white space, with a company that's now twice the size, before the end of the year. In markets that move that fast, waterfall planning just doesn't cut it. Speed, agility and the willingness to pivot when the moment's right are more valuable than any number of Gantt charts and point-and-arrow critical path schedules.

The core organization has many of the resources that may need to be leveraged to launch and grow a new business, including skills, domain expertise, sales and distribution channels, brands and data – probably a vast amount of data.

What it is unlikely to have is the entrepreneurial flair and expertise you'll need, or the cutting-edge tech know-how. Any potential entrepreneurs working there are likely to have had those instincts drilled out of them or submerged for years under the disciplines and KPIs of an operation that is optimized for efficiency, rather than exponential growth. The cultural differences between the two parts of your hybrid organization, the 'exploit' side and the 'explore' side, are too great to ignore. Only by adopting the disciplined, purposeful framework of the Entrepreneurial Operating Model can you reasonably hope to create a situation where you can get the full benefits of the corporate venture building process.

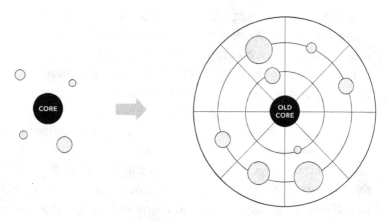

Bringing structure to the ecosystem

The graphic above shows how this transformational process works. On the left is what typically happens today. The corporation has a few digital projects, but they are not connected to one another and lack strategic alignment with the core's organization. To create more momentum, the core organization must take the lead role in coordinating the activities of its offspring and ensuring that all the available synergies are put to good use. This orchestrating role requires a real sense of commitment and focus. The core's orchestrator is the Entrepreneurial Growth Board we discussed earlier.

OUR KEY RECOMMENDATIONS FOR YOU:

- Start by analysing what your strengths are. What are you uniquely able to do? Which assets, which may seem dull or irrelevant now, could be particularly valuable in a new setting? With corporate venture building, these assets can be combined with the talents of seasoned entrepreneurs to help you operate in complex industries where no VC-backed or self-funded start-up would dare to show its face.

- Make sure everything you do is strategically relevant, so everything contributes to the larger picture. Set up a board – the Entrepreneurial Growth Board – to guide developments and protect the fledgling business from the habits and vested interests of the core organization. Board members should include entrepreneurs, as well as top executives.

- Corporate venture building takes commitment and involvement from the parent organization's senior leadership. Those running the new corporate ventures must be guaranteed face-to-face time with the corporation's top brass so they can properly explain new developments and opportunities.

- Get the right people on board for now. The needs of early stage businesses can change fast, in a matter of months. Start small, hire carefully and don't try to plan staffing too far ahead. Who you employ now will define who you can get in later.

- Be ready to act on various dimensions, as shown in the Corporate Venture Circle, in parallel. As a minimum, aim to be smart about the team culture, cover off the regulatory angles, get the incentives right and create seamless links between new digital businesses and the corporate core to ensure good communication and easy access to needed assets. Then you can start talking about a mission, a purpose and the higher goal of making a positive impact in the world.

ENERGY MEETS INNOVATION

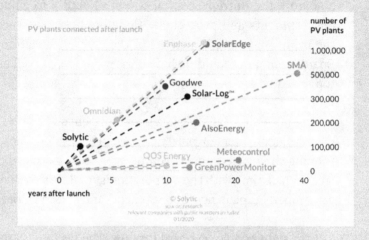

Global solar PV market 2020:
Solytic hits 100,000 plants after two years

If the renewables sector was a sport, Johannes Burgard and his Solytic team would be playing in the Champions League by now. Leading the way towards digital transformation in the sector with integrity, positivity and a strong sense of purpose, Burgard and his team have made Solytic the fastest-growing solar software company in the world.

Solytic provides a fine practical example of the corporate venture building process in action, having created a revolutionary high-tech solar power monitoring company with an eight-digit price tag in just two years.

Everybody's talking about the switch to green energy and decentralized electricity production these days. But no one has a bigger incentive to do it fast and get it right than one of Europe's largest power companies, Vattenfall.

So how does a giant, century-old utility find the ideas, inspiration and agility to turn on a dime and begin acting like a Silicon Valley start-up?

Vattenfall is huge. It is wholly owned by the Swedish government and it's a major energy supplier across northern Europe, with 14 million customers in Denmark, Finland, Germany, the Netherlands and the UK, as well as in its home country.

But despite its eco-friendly, green-sounding name (Vattenfall is the Swedish for waterfall), the company knows it has a long way to go to clean up its act. Originally it was all about hydro power, but from the 1970s onwards it built nuclear power stations and fossil fuel generating capacity on a large scale. Now it is concentrating on moving to cleaner, greener generation methods. It has a rapidly developing solar power business and there are now more than a thousand on- and offshore wind turbines in five European countries under the Vattenfall brand.

Vattenfall's ambition is to move to CO_2-free generation and create the possibility of fossil fuel-free living within one generation.

"We want to help people be 'climate smarter' in their living," says Gunnar Groebler, the senior VP with responsibility for all Vattenfall's wind and solar activities and a member of the executive management board. "We are on a journey. We don't have all the answers.

But we're making good progress as a company –
for ourselves, for our customers, for our suppliers,
and for society."

There's a long road ahead, but Vattenfall has not been
too proud to ask for help in developing new ideas and
new businesses to support its efforts in solar and wind.
It was realistic about its lack of experience with new
digital technologies. The company recognized that
people who had spent their entire careers in a state-
owned electricity company were not necessarily tuned
in to the brave new world of entrepreneurial start-ups,
venture capital and platform business models.

"We saw how digitization was changing other industries," says Juliane Schulze, who leads Vattenfall's
business development efforts in renewables. "But we
didn't have a clue how it would affect energy markets
in the future."

Neither, of course, did any of us at FoundersLane. But
we know how to put in the legwork to research and
explore a new field and we do know how to generate
new ideas once we have the necessary background
knowledge. So when Schulze and her Director of Business Development, Claus Wattendrup, got in touch with
Felix and asked if we might be able to help, we were
very interested in comparing notes with them.

Vattenfall had already set up an innovation platform it
called green:field, aimed at growing new businesses in
the areas of solar photovoltaic (PV) generation and batteries. But what started out in October 2016 as a series
of advice sessions with Felix and his FoundersLane

co-founders, Michael Stephanblome and Andreas von Oettingen, about establishing a governance model for digital transformation initiatives at green:field soon turned into a more significant partnership.

Initially, Vattenfall asked us to develop a digital operating model and a digital advisory group that would hold monthly board-level meetings and help the company's executives improve their understanding of digital issues and act more quickly on new opportunities.

Within two months, we had set up a digital steering committee, known as the Board of Entrepreneurs. This was composed of four senior people from Vattenfall, led by Groebler, and three people on the Founders-Lane side – Felix, Michael and our close friend and ally, Markus Fuhrmann, famous for having co-founded Delivery Hero and several other successful start-ups.

The main task of the Board of Entrepreneurs was to look at the various paths open to the energy giant in its search for significant new ventures.

Vattenfall could build its new businesses from within, as internal start-ups, which would enable them to draw on existing know-how but be less ideal when blue sky thinking was needed and market competitiveness was at a premium.

Or it could build partnerships based on joint projects with external start-ups to create new technologies for use within the company's core operations, identify customer needs and build pilot products. Alternatively, it might choose to make acquisitions to get its hands on new businesses, new technologies or a set of skills and talents that were not available internally.

Yet within a few weeks the emphasis changed. Vattenfall decided it wanted to work directly with us and it signed up for a 12-week White Space Garage idea-generating project. This quickly produced exciting results and led on to a full-scale corporate venture building engagement, which eventually prompted the formation of Solytic.

STRUCTURED DATA GETS MORE OUT OF SOLAR

The desperately needed change to a carbon-neutral world won't happen without an immense expansion of power generation by solar plants. But for this energy revolution to gain momentum, the cost of generating solar power must fall, and keep on coming down, year after year.

From sourcing to recycling, the solar PV value chain is rapidly digitizing. Today's solar installations pay for themselves over a period of eight to 15 years, and the aim must be to reduce costs, keep panels going longer and improve performance and reliability, with automated monitoring and predictive maintenance helping to identify potential outages long before they actually happen.

Today, Solytic is the world's fastest-growing solar software start-up. It took less than two years to pass the milestone of 100,000 PV plants, with 2.5GW in decentralized assets serving B2B customers from Mexico to Japan. Its goal now is to reach 1 million plants by 2023.

The key to this success has undoubtedly been the corporate venture building model, based on a joint team drawn from Vattenfall and FoundersLane. In the first few weeks of the collaboration, as the team worked its way through the White Space Garage process, a dozen different business ideas were explored. This led to a modest portfolio of three promising themes – using real-time software analytics to boost energy yields, deploying advanced AI to improve maintenance and asset management, and enlisting crowdfunding techniques to raise cash for renewable energy projects.

Even at this early stage, a great deal of research was going on behind the scenes. Team members made a thousand calls, talked to 80 experts and conducted 60 detailed interviews, and they were soon able to identify several major inefficiencies affecting the performance of PV installations around the world.

Degradation of the solar panels, they discovered, meant that PV plants steadily lost power, while operators had no reliable way of knowing how well their systems were working, taking into account factors like the weather, panel angles, positioning and the performance of the inverters that convert DC to AC current.

Within a few weeks, it was clear the team was on to something big. By the end of the second phase of the formal corporate venture building process, the minimum viable product validation stage, the losses caused by PV panel and inverter degradation had been identified as the main problem facing operators. There was a definite market opportunity for a digital solution based on data analytics that could increase revenues by improving asset management.

The new project was initially dubbed Phoenix, a classically sunny name, but one that said very little about what the solution involved. It was soon changed to Solytic, a neat combination of the ideas of solar and analytics. As the team dug deeper, it identified a potential market for solar monitoring that was worth tens of billions in Europe alone. If the owners of PV installations, who were losing money every day of the year, could be given the tools they needed to achieve better performance and revenues, Solytic would be in business.

The key to doing it, from a technical point of view, was the combination of specialist artificial intelligence and the Internet of Things know-how our team was able to bring to the party. Solytic creates a benchmark profile for each individual solar installation – basically a digital twin of the actual PV asset, taking into account a massive number of data points from similar installations elsewhere – and uses this to track the efficiency of the system.

If a PV panel is performing badly or an inverter is faulty, Solytic flags this up in real time and advises on remedial action. In the future, it will even support predictive maintenance, telling owners in advance when an individual panel or inverter is likely to fail, based on the failure records of thousands of similar units, so that a replacement can be lined up or even installed before the fault occurs. A solar panel that goes dark produces no revenue at all, so this is valuable information.